The Wide Awake Kids Club

Simple Solutions for Knackered Parents

Fi Star-Stone

Copyright © 2019 Fi Star-Stone

Illustrations and cover design by Betsy Stone

All rights reserved.

ISBN: 9781092720793

CONTENTS

3

For my family and friends who
support me and my crazy schemes and dreams.
Thank you, I love you lots.

To my wonderful readers - sorry this one took so long!
Blame my family, friends for keeping me busy!

'Sing me to sleep,
Sing me to sleep,
I'm tired and I,
I want to go to bed'

The Smiths

INTRODUCTION

Hello lovely face!

Firstly, thanks for purchasing this little sleep guide of mine. I really hope the gentle techniques, tips and information, help your family create healthy sleep habits that last, because, let's face it - sleep is one of the most important needs in life. Without sleep, we begin to suffer both physically and mentally, (car keys in the fridge anyone?)

If your little love is a fully fledged member of *The Wide Awake kids Club* - don't worry, you're not alone! Sleepless nights aren't just reserved for the new-parent brigade and their little newborn bundles! With tech taking over, modern day stresses and complicated lives, I'm getting more and more help requests from families with *older* children struggling with bedtimes.

From wide-awakers that refuse to go to bed, to midnight gang bed invaders, I've been overwhelmed with requests for solutions to solving bedtime issues. So, I decided to write this little book in the hope it'll help families everywhere get better, healthier sleep.

You've likely bought this sleep guide because you're totally knackered and want a quick-fix solution to your child's sleep issues. I'll be brutally honest - there is no quick fix when it comes to sleep. It takes time, patience and a whole lot of consistency.

Without wanting to sound like a total 'expert bore-off,' being consistent and working as a team, is crucial to make any of the techniques in this book work. Everyone involved in your child's life needs to be on the same page. All of you need to follow the same plan, same rules and to all be consistent, otherwise it just won't work.

You don't need to read this book cover to cover, you can of course skip to the good bits, or the chapters you feel are relevant to your child, but I honestly think if you read it all the way through, the tips - and thoughts behind them, will make so much more sense.

Without another word of ramble, let's begin the journey to better sleep for you all.

Chapter One
Why is sleep important and how much does my child need?

As parents, we all have, at some stage, known how it feels to be sleep deprived and how unwell it makes us feel. We also know we need decent sleep to live a happy, healthy life. But what does sleep actually do?

According to the *National Institute of Neurological Disorders and Stroke* (NINDS,) Sleep affects almost every type of tissue and system in the body - from the brain, heart, and lungs to metabolism, immune function, mood, and disease resistance.

Research shows that a chronic lack of sleep, or getting poor quality sleep, increases the risk of disorders including high blood pressure, cardiovascular disease, diabetes, depression, and obesity.

The Stages of Sleep

According to *NINDS* there are two basic types of sleep: Rapid eye movement (REM) sleep and non-REM sleep - which has several different stages. Each is linked to specific brain waves and neuronal activity.

You cycle through all stages of non-REM and REM sleep several times during a typical night, with increasingly longer, deeper REM periods occurring toward morning.

Stage 1 non-REM sleep is the changeover from wakefulness to sleep. During this short period (lasting several minutes) of relatively light sleep, your heartbeat, breathing, and eye movements slow down and your muscles relax. This is also the time when the muscles jerk, followed by a falling sensation that jolts you back into consciousness. This experience is known as hypnic myoclonia. (If you can say that first attempt, unlike me - then you get a gold star!) During this time your brain waves also begin to slow down from their daytime wakefulness patterns.

Stage 2 non-REM sleep is a period of light sleep before you enter a deeper sleep. Your heartbeat and breathing slow even more, and muscles relax even further. Your body temperature drops and eye movements stop. Brain wave activity slows but is marked by brief bursts of electrical activity. interestingly, you spend more of your repeated sleep cycles in stage 2 sleep, than in other sleep stages.
Stage 3 non-REM sleep is the the magic stuff. The period of deep sleep that you need to feel refreshed in the morning. It occurs in longer periods during the first half of the night.

Your heartbeat and breathing slow to their lowest levels during this sleep, your muscles are relaxed and it may be difficult to wake you up. If you try to wake your child up when they are in stages three or four, they will most likely be disoriented and groggy for a few minutes after they awake.

Even though there is no muscle movement during this time - the muscles still have the ability to function. These are the stages when children sometimes experience nightmares, bedwetting and sleepwalking.

REM sleep first occurs about 90 minutes after falling asleep. Your eyes move rapidly from side to side behind closed eyelids. Mixed frequency brain wave activity becomes closer to that seen in wakefulness. Your breathing becomes faster and irregular, and your heart rate and blood pressure increase to near waking levels.

Most of your dreaming occurs during REM sleep, (although some can also occur in non-REM sleep.) Your arm and leg muscles become temporarily paralysed, which prevents you from acting out your dreams.

So with all of this in mind, how much shut-eye do our little loves actually need and how much are they actually getting?

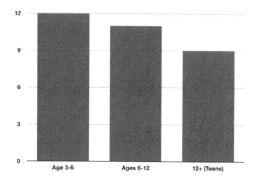

Every child is different, but as a general guide and based on Based on NHS guidelines this translates as:

· Ages 3 - 6 Between 10-12 hours

· Ages 6 -12 between 10-11 hours

It's important to note here that these sleep patterns are based on children who don't have any underlying medical conditions or any additional physical or developmental needs.

How much sleep is my child *actually* getting?

Looking at the previous chat - think about the hours that are needed, then think about what time your child is going to bed and staying awake until. It really is an eye-opener when you total it all up.

I'll admit to some nights being totally shattered myself, having done the whole bedtime routine, left them reading as they do each night to settle, then forgetting to shout up that it's 'lights out time' to find my eldest (age 9 as I write this,) still reading at 9.30pm. Oops.

I think most parents I talk to and help, don't realise how *very little* sleep their children are getting each night when they add up the hours. I recently asked my social media followers and the families I work with, what time their children went to bed and the results were interesting.

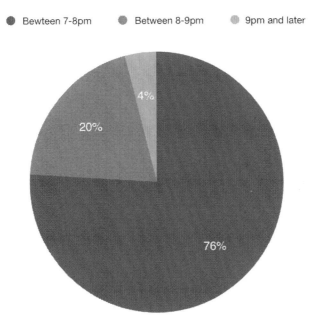

● Bewteen 7-8pm   ● Between 8-9pm   ● 9pm and later

4%

20%

76%

*Survey of 1000 parents January 2019 on Fi Star-Stone twitter, Instagram and Facebook page 'Childcare is Fun!'

While it looks from the chart that the majority of children had pretty good bedtimes, (the main bedtime being 7-8pm), when I asked parents to work out what hours their children *actually* slept the results were interesting.

Around a quarter of parents who took part in the survey told me their children went to bed with tech (tablets or smartphones.) A small percentage of parents said their children played on games consoles in bed, while over half said their children read in bed to settle for the evening.

A large number of parents admitted their children were still awake up to *two hours* after they had gone to bed! So, although their children went to bed at a reasonable 7-8pm, they weren't actually getting to sleep until near 9-10pm.

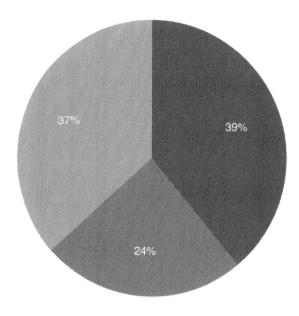

● 9-10 hours plus per night   ● 8-9 hours per night   ● less than 8 hours per night

*Survey of 1000 parents January 2019 on Fi Star-Stone twitter, Instagram and Facebook page 'Childcare is Fun!'

Some parents even admitted to finding their children still awake when they went to bed themselves, around 11.30pm most evenings, but these were (mainly) the children that went to bed with tech or played on games consoles.

The *easy life* isn't always the best life!

I get it, as a parent myself, I do understand that it's often easier choosing the *easy life* rather than arguing and stressing at bedtime - especially if you've had an exhausting day.

Other than battling bedtime while knackered, many parents told me it's easy to hand over the tech as a 'bedtime babysitter' and it often keeps their children not only get into bed but stay there.

These 'sleep band-aids' work - of course they do, but they don't create good sleep routines for life.

I truly believe healthy sleep is as important as feeding children the right food, protecting them from the bad stuff on the internet, and keeping them safe when out and about. Sleep is so important for their well being - so I truly think it's our job as parents to do the best by them that we can.

I'm not saying of course, that letting your children fall asleep with tech means you are a bad parent - far from it. We all do what works for us at the time, but I suspect you'd not have purchased this book if you were happy with your child's sleep habits and that really, you want to change things to create better sleep skills without the use of tech to fall asleep to every night.

Sleep deprived kids = Grumpy, non-focused kids!

With the majority of children waking up at an average time of 7am or earlier on school days, most children get an average of 8 hours sleep a night instead of the recommended 10-12 hours per night for children aged 3-12.

Add that up each week, and you're looking at, (based on the lower 10 hour recommendation,) 14 hours of missed, valuable, sleep each week.

Knowing that sleep is needed for growth, development and that a lack of sleep can cause moodiness, lack of concentration, lethargy and in time can cause health problems - it's something to really think about isn't it?

With a lack of sleep, or constant broken sleep, many children are loosing out on essential 'body maintenance and repair' each night. What I mean by that is, poor sleep skills mean many children loose out on REM sleep - the magic part of sleep that stimulates the brain regions used in learning.

REM sleep begins with signals from an area at the base of the brain called the pons. These signals travel to a brain region called the thalamus, which relays them to the cerebral cortex - the outer layer of the brain that is responsible for learning, thinking, and organising information.

Not only that, during the deep states of NREM sleep (Non Rapid Eye Movement,) blood supply to the muscles is increased, energy is restored, tissue growth and repair occur, and important hormones are released for growth and development.

I'm not trying to worry you, or make you feel bad - that's not what I'm about. I truly think that understanding how sleep cycles work and how valuable sleep is, will help you to have the right mindset when fixing any sleep issues you are facing.

It's so easy to just give in and take the easy route to bedtime with tech, TV, giving in to whatever-just-gets-them-into-bed-damn-it! but really, it's all quick fixes - and actually, with determination, consistency and a whole lot of patience in only a short time things can and will change.

So my friend, if you are ready, and you want to get better, healthier night-times and ditch the stressful, can't-cope-anymore bedtime battles, let's look at some of the main causes of children joining the *Wide Awake Kids Club* and how you can help them ditch their membership.

Chapter Two
The Midnight Gang - what to do when your child refuses to go to bed (or wakes up in the night and hops in with you!)

You've likely been there a million times before, the lovely chilled wind-down time, watching TV with your little love? You've given the *five minutes til' bedtime* warning, and all is calm until the five minutes is up.

Then, every-excuse-in-the-world tactics start, the tears and sometimes the tantrums too, and so begins the bedtime battle night after night that leaves you all stressed, upset and quite frankly, bloody knackered? We've all been there haven't we? Yes, even me 'the expert' with my shiny degree and qualifications, and all the years experience, I get the bad bedtimes too - but it's fixable. I promise.

If your bed hopper or bed refuser is giving you grief, read on my friend, read on.

Routine is the magic key for a better bedtime

I know I say it a lot. I said it loads in my last book, *The Baby Bedtime book - Say goodnight to Sleepless nights*, in my TV and radio interviews, in my parenting emails and on social media, oh my do I say it all the time, but *'routine really is the magic key!'* Without it - there's no structure or consistency and even for adults, this can cause major issues when it comes to good sleep habits and better bedtimes.

Routine is the magic key! It really is. That old favourite bedtime routine that you had with your baby or toddler, has probably been long forgotten right?

The regular 6pm bath, milk and bedtime cosy routine? It slipped into something like 8pm after football training, quick showers, a miss of the bedtime story as it's getting late and you've still not had your own dinner? Perhaps it's more like an 8.30pm after dance class and bath, or the 9pm main rush upstairs when you didn't realise the time because you'd been distracted on your phone (come on - we've all done it) and they sure as hell weren't going to tell you it was late and time for bed! Sound about right?

So as boring and mundane as it sounds - *routine is the magic key* to a good night's sleep. Good bedtime habits work. Fact.

Not right away, nothing is that simple in parenting, but with consistency, patience and determination, a regular bedtime and a regular bedtime routine, will have your child on their way to the land of nod, rather than wide-awake-party-in-your-room at 11pm every night!

Routine is the magic key - but it's hard!

Life is busy and routines are complicated - I get it! I'm a mum of two and as a family we juggle Brownies, football, golf, Great Nanna Wednesday visits (she's 92 if you're asking,) and numerous other appointments, which means sometimes we are not home until 8pm!

Despite these crazy after-school evenings, one thing I try my best to follow - is routine. And it works. Routine is the magic key - but it's hard! It is *really* hard sometimes to keep at it but it works. How do I know it works? Well, not only are my two epic sleepers the majority of the time, in the holidays, when I let it slack and routine isn't followed, then it all goes wrong!

A break in the routine and I find myself struggling with a non-sleeper, or the nightmares will begin (more on this later,) but I know it's all easily fixed with a little hard work and consistency. *Back to the routine* fixes all.

This dedication to the routine often means training my husband to do the same! (He's good cop in our house) - if you have a good cop too, here's a little side-note here lovely faces - you have to work as a team with your partner if you have one. Routine will be the routine you have decided together.

Yes I know as a parenting advisor I advise both parents to be on the same page in all areas of parenting - but in reality? Come on - you know in every house there is *usually* one parent that is often a little easier to bend and break than the other. In our house - it's Daddy aka my husband Rich. (Sorry hun - true story.)

Anyway, my point here is you have to have each others backs when it comes to the bedtime battle - support each other and be consistent when it comes to bedtime. *Note to Rich - are you reading this? ;0)

In his defence - Rich often gets home at bedtime, they're so excited to see him - but bedtime is bedtime, and although everyone is happy and excited (apart from me trying to calm them down for bedtime) - we need to stick to the plan! Maybe you have this issue too? (If you're single parenting - firstly - I salute you, you guys do an amazing job and I think you are brilliant. Secondly, this will be more in your favour as there's nobody else giving different rules or breaking the consistency.)

So your partner comes home from the office/blogger event/footy/yoga/band practice/filming/radio show (whatever they come back from) - and you've got a nice calm setting going on. Partner walks in all excited and BOOM - they're all fired up and ready for the day, not for bed thanks-very-much parents! You both do it I bet? Whoever gets in last? (I get it! I've even been guilty of this too!)

But no matter the excitement - quit the grand entrance at bedtime. You have to work together on this every time. Calm, consistent, bedtime. Chill.

Whatever time for bed you have decided will work for you as a family - stick to it. Even the babysitter needs-in on the bedtime routine. Grandparents, Nannies, Au-pairs, Aunties or Uncles - anyone involved with your child's bedtime needs to be on the same page otherwise it just won't work. One mess-up in the grand-bedtime-plan and you're back to night one of trying to fix it. Not even joking.

These things take time - you need to be strong and take the time to deal with the issues rather than patch over them with bedtime-plasters (aka iPads/TV/Bribery!)

An epic bedtime game plan

You need a good plan to work this bedtime nonsense out. Kids are smart. Smarter than babies and toddlers who follow routines quite quickly.

Older children are wise, they are good at making excuses and they are quick to change their own game plan to get what they want. Kids are epic.

I love children, I love their little minds and how quickly they can adapt and change their bedtime tricks to get their own way. I did it myself as a child (sorry mum!) I bet you did too.

I love the creativity that my two come out with sometimes as bedtime-stalling tactics. My favourites include: *'My pillow is too hot!'* or *'my clock is ticking too loudly!'* They've even tried a few heart-tug quotes in their time *'but I just miss you so much Mummy'* nice try kid - bedtime now though thanks very much, I'm about to embark on my *'Game of Thrones* journey!' (As I write this - I still haven't seen an episode! I'm fixing this the minute this book goes to print as everyone keeps going on about it! Please don't Judge my lack of GOT experience.)

Anyway, I digress; Let's face it, most children don't want to go to bed through a fear of missing out. (FOMO - for the cool parents out there!)

Remember yourself as a child? That plead for an extra five minutes? The protest stomp up the stairs? Think back to that, when dealing with your own little loves and how you can perhaps make bedtime more interesting (and no - not the iPad!)

Making bedtime more fun!

Make their bedroom a place they want to go to at the end of the day. Fill it with things that are aesthetically pleasing - their favourite band posters, or TV characters perhaps, or their favourite colours on the wall and quilt cover.

Don't make bedtime an *'into-bed-lights-out'* time right away - this will just make your child's battle bedtime brain commence, when it doesn't really need to. Instead, let them read in bed for a while to settle - it's a perfect way to relax both the body and mind before bed.

Don't be tempted to let them watch TV or go on any tech.

Switch off is best off!

I'm coining that one - I've checked all the socials and nobody has taken it! Hey I might even hashtag it. #SwitchOffisBestOff for a better, healthier sleep. (I need to remind myself of this often as I'm guilty of midnight scrolling on my phone!)

For those of you with the tech savvy, TV loving, kids out there - you will not love this next bit. In order to get that brain and body ready for sleep, you have to be a bit of a boring, not-very-much-liked parent here. SWITCH OFF at least half an hour before the bedtime routine begins. (An hour is even better if you dare!)

To avoid drama here, give a ten-minute warning before switch-off and before the bedtime routine begins.

Let them know in ten minutes it's switch-off time to get ready for bed. As a parent myself with a little Xbox player who needs a warning to finish the level he's on before switching off, I do understand how tricky this can be. The pleads to *'just complete one more thing, please mama can I? Please?'* has to be ignored, but remember - they need the ten-minute switch off warning, or expect epic grumpiness and another likely failed bedtime.

Try setting a timer with an alarm sound so they understand the ten minutes isn't one of your usual made-up ten minutes. (We all do it!) This works so much better in our house as it's both a visual and sensory acceptance that it's time for bed.

What if they refuse to go to bed?

Ah come on lovely face! You got this.

Firm but fair is my motto - give the ten minute warnings, then if they refuse to switch off, they lose time on their games console/screen time the next day. It's not bribery or blackmail - it's an incentive. incentives work.

'But what if they refuse to go to bed?'

If they play by the bedtime rules, they get to play again tomorrow. It's that simple. Give them the choice rather than making it a nagging battle.

Ignore the pleads that they will *'loose their place in the game,'* remember some games are highly addictive - (don't get me started on kids playing certain games underage,) you have to be the parent here and just switch it off. If they lose the point of their game - it's really not a big deal and they will learn next time to switch off when you asked them nicely to. Firm but fair mate. Firm but fair.

It's the same with the tidying up refusal, music switched off, whatever activity they are up to. Give them the choice to switch off/tidy up or lose out tomorrow. They are not toddlers anymore, so let them make the decision.

Give them the right incentive and they will more than likely do as requested. You are not the ogre here - you are giving them the gift of sleep, the power of the nap - the magic stuff that helps them be the best they can be. Remember, sleep is one of the most important needs in life, so don't feel bad for helping your child to be the best they can be.

Talk about sleep

Talking about sleep is really beneficial when it comes to creating better bedtimes.

Chat regularly to your children about how important sleep is, and how we need to recharge - just like batteries do in the games controller or the laptop. It helps to discuss it and to make it a topic of conversation, rather than the whole *DO AS YOUR TOLD* retro-style thinking.

Encourage bedtime with a reward system for positive bedtime behaviour - these can be really handy if you're really knackered and need a quick fix to a situation spinning out of control.

Reward systems work

They've probably outgrown the old sticker chart now (if they haven't and still love them - stick with it! Pah! See what I did there? *Stick* with it?)

Older children are often more into cash rewards or treats. Sad but true! Use this as a positive and invest some time into making and discussing my rather well loved *'Reward Jar of Awesome!'*

'A pebble in for positive behaviour, a pebble out for negative - works really well towards an end week treat'

To make a *Reward Jar of Awesome* you'll need:

- A large jar

- Buttons or small pebbles

- A firm but fair and consistent attitude

How to make and use your *Reward Jar of Awesome!*

1. Fill the jar with a few pebbles or buttons, (the ones already in the jar are there incase you need to remove some before you've added any! This often happens in the first trial!)

2. Explain to your child what the jar is all about. Talk about behaviour that's great and what's not so great! (Refusing to go to bed, for example, means buttons will be removed.)

3. Every time there is good behaviour (including epic bedtime behaviour) pop a button in the jar. When there are 20 (or however many you decide) a treat is gained! It doesn't have to be anything expensive - perhaps extra time on the Xbox on a weekend, a favourite magazine, or a trip to the movies - whatever you think your child might want to work towards.

4. Every time the behaviour is negative, you remove a button. You'll find they learn and begin to like the idea very quickly. Behaviour is often improved considerably after only a few 'button removals.'

5. Remind and reward all the time - if you can see something is about to happen, remind them about the jar. Often a reminder is enough to change behaviour!

6. Respond to good behaviour in an exaggerated way, make a big deal of going to bed on time or staying in their bed all night.

7. It's a really simple idea and one that has worked for hundreds of families that have come to me with kids that just refuse to go to, or stay in bed.

Other reward charts with stickers work too - point systems for treats, extra hours doing something they love, or even money for each successful bedtime (10p a night towards their pocket money for example or however much you decide as a family.)

Rewards systems work only when you are consistent, so don't get lazy, and don't use them as idle threats - follow each thing through and you'll son see a change in bedtime behaviour.

What do I do about my early-morning bed invader?

Feeling shattered and like a zombie due to your early 5am bed-invader? Perhaps you have a midnight gang member that invites themselves into your sleep haven each night?

Let's face it - between 5 and 6am in the morning it's technically still night-time, so being woken at this time can make you feel zombie-like because you've likely been woken from your deep-sleep state. Imagine how you would feel with an extra hour or two in the morning instead of your 5am start! Like a totally new person I bet!

As a parent myself - I know how hard it is getting by on very little sleep. Mine were born less than a year apart, so when illness strikes in our house - it's like tag team for my two taking it in turn to keep me awake with high temps or sickness bugs and my days spent in Mombie mode craving for bedtime.

Early starts mount up - even just an hour a day woken at 5 can have an affect on your wellbeing over time. Too many interrupted nights and you'll find your cosy Netflix evenings are soon replaced with ridiculously early nights in bed playing catch-up. Sleep is all you can think about right?

Fixing these bed-invader habits is essential for your own sleep health as well as your little one's.

What time should my child be sleeping in until?

Every child is different, but generally, by the time your little one is 6 months old, it's pretty reasonable to expect sleeping to last until at least 6am, if not 7am. So now they are much older, 7am, if not 8am, are perfectly reasonable expectations. Of course this depends on a variety of things - one very important problem being clock changes. (You can read all about that in the *Ch, ch, ch Changes* Chapter!)

Routine is the magic key!

OMG. She's said it again. I know - I'm banging on about routine again, but it really is important, and without it your child can become overtired. As crazy as it sounds, one of the biggest causes of sleep problems, including early waking and bed invasions, is in

22

'Encouraging your child to read a book before bed,

sets up the mind for adventures

and really relaxes their mind.'

fact over-tiredness! When your child doesn't sleep enough, the brain releases the hormone cortisol. This can stimulate your child into feeling more awake and alert when they should be sleepy, so get (and keep) that awesome bedtime routine and you'll soon be back to better bedtimes.

The perfect bedtime routine

What time are you putting your child to bed? Anything later than 7pm can result in over-tiredness too, especially for little schoolers (key stage 1) who like all children, need their sleep to function well at school.

Many parents think that keeping kids up late will make them sleep later - wrong! It actually has the opposite effect. A healthy bedtime for school age kids, is anything from 7pm – 8pm so go by your own little one and look for the tired signs. (Rubbing eyes, starting to get a little cranky or twirling their hair, sucking their thumb.) Act on those signs right away rather than waiting until they are so tired the bedtime battle commences!

The perfect bedtime routine is best started at least half an hour before they are getting into bed. As mentioned before, stop the days activities with a five or ten minute warning to avoid strops.

Bath-time = Chill time!

Baths can really help an overtired child and really help with wind-down time.

You may have ditched the regular evening baths from the baby and toddler days, in favour of showers. But if your super-sleeper has suddenly turned into a wide-awaker, try starting each evening by running them a nice warm bath. Pop some lavender oil in to create a calming effect, then help them get into fresh PJ's, teeth brushed and into bed with either a story or a book to read themselves.

Encouraging your child to read a book before bed sets up the mind for adventures and really relaxes their mind. According to a study conducted in 2009 by researchers at the University of Sussex, opening a book before you go to bed can help you cope with insomnia.

The study showed that even as little as six minutes of reading, reduces stress by 68%, clearing the mind and preparing the body for sleep.

Dr. David Lewis, a psychologist and author of the study, says *'A book is more than merely a distraction, but an active engaging of the imagination, one that causes you to enter an altered state of consciousness.'*

My two love books and sometimes my eldest Betsy, loves to go to bed early because she's had a new book from the library or bought as a gift. Her favourite author is Jacqueline Wilson - and I've know her to even go to bed at 6pm to indulge in a reading adventure and finish the book two hours later!

Betsy thought it might be nice to share her favourite five books with you - incase your little bookworms might like to have a read of them too!

They're aimed at ages 8+ and are wonderful reads;

1. Dancing the Charleston - Jacqueline Wilson

2. Tracy Beaker - Jacqueline Wilson

3. Ella on the Outside - Cath Howe

4. The Magic Faraway Tree - Enid Blyton

5. Pippi Longstocking books - Astrid Lindgren

My son Oscar also loves to read, he absolutely loves David Walliams books - and here are his top five favourite bedtime reads:

1. Gangsta Granny - by David Williams

2. Billionaire Boy - David Walliams

3. The Smartest Giant in Town - Julia Donaldson

4. Dogman - Dav Pilkey

5. The Twits - Roald Dahl

Check book content!

When choosing stories and books for children, check the content, check the images and check it's nothing too frightening that's going to keep them up worrying!

Sometimes parents just assume because a book is in the right age range on a bookshelf - it'll be OK, but some children don't cope as well with some things, that others might - so go by your own child. My two love The Hobbit and Harry Potter, but it may be a little too scary for others of the same age.

Once your little love is settled into bed ready to read or settle for the night, ensure they are comfortable and feel reassured.

A way of getting them to talk to you and get anything out that they may be worried about, is my popular *'One rubbish, Three Awesomes'* technique.

One rubbish, three awesomes!

The reason behind using this technique at bedtime is because it's when children really want to talk! You know the stalling tactics of delaying bedtime? Well this technique means you're both getting what you want! They get that extra ten-minutes staying up chatting to you, and you get to find out about the bad and good in their day! This can really help with bedtime worries because it's getting any worry, big or small, off their chest before bedtime and making the mind lighter for sleep.

With this technique, always tart with the negative. This is the one rubbish thing about their day. You can encourage this by sharing a negative about your day followed by your three awesomes. It can be as simple as *'I was late to work today'* as a negative and *'seeing you at the end of my day, eating a donut and going for a nice walk'* as the three positives! (That sounds like quite an awesome day doesn't it? I'm all about the donuts!)

Remember; Always start with the rubbish and end on a positive. The important thing to remember is to start with the bad and end on a happy. That way they'll fall asleep thinking about the positive moments in their day.

With older children who are reluctant to talk, (pre-teens or teenagers,) invest in a 'communication journal' - a simple notepad or journal where you can both write your thoughts for each other to read. Let them know they can write anything they want, even if it's bad, and they won't get into trouble. It's a great way of you telling each other anything you're upset or worried about, and keeping the lines of communication open. Some things are easier to write down that speak out loud.

It's so important to talk to your children, no matter what their age. This simple technique is a great way of having that communication ongoing in the family and can settle worried minds at bedtime.

Fears of the dark

For those with night fears or worries invest in a night light and offer lots of reassurance. (For tips on night fears you can head on over to the '*bumps in the night*' chapter!)

It's really important to mention here, that once you have started the bedtime routine, (baths and PJ's and teeth) to not be tempted to go back downstairs and watch TV.

Not only are you giving yourself an extra battle to start the whole routine again, screens stimulate little ones and ideally shouldn't be watched half an hour before bedtime. By sticking to ta good bedtime routine - you'll notice a change in only a few days. I promise.

Consistency is key

Start as you mean to go on. If you are ready to start a new bedtime routine to get back to better sleep, you have to be consistent. This means everyone in the house following the same page.

I know I've already mentioned this - but also remember if your child stays over at grandparents to let them know the routine too. (You listening Nanna and Poppops? Those 9pm bedtimes are not ideal!)

Paha! Only kidding. Grandparents get to do whatever they like. I think it's called 'parent payback.'

The Midnight Gang bed-invader

If your child keeps coming into your room in the middle of the night, it's important to walk them back to their room quietly and calmly without conversation right away. It's not mean - it's simply because any chat will stimulate and wake them from their sleepy fogginess and it's unlikely you'll get them settled again.

Walk them back to their room, simply say 'it's bed time' and leave the room. Keep repeating this, as exhausting as it may be, it'll only take a few nights to work.

Don't be tempted to let them into your bed and snuggle - as lovely as that is, that'll just become a new habit that's hard to break. (Of course if you want to do that - you can! There's nothing nicer than a morning snuggle with a little one, but I expect you wouldn't be reading this if you didn't mind doing that every night or morning!)

Invest in a bedtime clock

I see many parents roll their eyes when I mention 'bedtime clocks' but honestly, they are a brilliant investment and work *if you put the work in*. I've lost count of the amount of times I've heard a parent say 'they don't work' as if they believe the clock itself has some magical ability to keep a child in bed.

It isn't the clock that does the work - the clock is just a bedtime tool! *You* have to put the effort in, and this usually only takes 3 nights of solid consistency and determination on your part.

Honestly! Put the work in and they really do work.

How does a bedtime clock actually help?

Bedtime clocks are set by you to show 'wake up time' and 'sleep time.'

There are many available out there at varying prices. You basically just set the times on the clock for bedtime and wake up time. Usually it'll show a different colour or a smiley face or a sun and moon to note the time of day.

When setting the times, be realistic. Remember as much as you fancy a 10am lie-in, (don't we all?) It's unlikely your child will co-operate and you're setting up for a clock fail before you've even began. Instead, think about the crazy times your child is waking you up each morning and work towards a reasonable time rather than going full-on first night.

For example, if they are waking at 5am every day, start with 5.30am as the acceptable wake up for the first day. (I know - don't panic, bear with me!)

Then two days later, and every other day, move it another ten minutes closer to the 'acceptable' morning wake-up time until you get to it. A reasonable time for an original 5am waker would be 6am. Stick with that for a couple of weeks, then move a little more. Don't go too far ahead if things are going well. Kids wake early - if they have gone from 5am to 6 or even 6.30am - that's a win. That's an extra 7 hours sleep each week you'll all be getting. Nice.

So remember - slowly slowly will get the job done. Fast-paced, quick-fixes simply don't work.

'Bedtime clocks are brilliant investment

and work if you put the work in!'

After the couple of weeks at 6am, and if they are playing along and it's all working out brilliantly, start moving it ten minutes every other day again until you get to 7am or whatever time you want. If it starts to go horribly wrong again - cut it back a little earlier. All children are different. Remember – most young children wake around

6.30am so again, don't expect a 10am lie-in! However, if you do manage a 10am lie-in everyday - please share with us all how the heck you did it, and what amazing life you have to get to stay in bed until 10am everyday. We all promise not to hate you.

Remind and reward

Use the clock as a reminder whenever there's a blip, or in the early days of using it, if they come into your room during bedtime hours. Point to the clock when you take them back to bed and say *'wait for the clock to say morning'* or something similar. Again, don't enter into long conversations, keep it brief.

If your *Wide Awake Club Member* manages to adjust and stick to the new routine - remind them how well they are doing and reward them with lots of praise or use the chart or jar shown in the previous chapter.

Older children can work towards a target – maybe a trip to the cinema for '5 good sleeps in a row.'

Make them feel like they are special and have achieved something great – because actually, they really have! As a parent you'll know the gift of sleep is priceless!

Chapter Three
The Counting Sheep Brigade - what to do when your child struggles to fall asleep!

There's so many reasons why your wide awake little poppet is struggling to fall asleep, and asking you for a long kist of things in intervals throughout your evening movie.

You know the drill *'I need a drink, I need a wee, my bed is lumpy'* and so on. These 'stalling tactics' have reasons behind them and need assessing, so cut a little slack, don't get cross and lose your cool. If you work towards a solution - it'll make it far less stressful.

You've probably realised by now that the *'JUST GO TO SLEEP!'* shouting upstairs rarely works, and it not only stresses your child out, it stresses you to the max too. There really is no need for tears at bedtime form anyone in the house - including you!

The ongoing battle of bedtime can wear down the patience of even the most chilled out parent, so solving this issue is as important as the whole getting them to bed in the first place.

Let's look into the many reasons why your wide-awaker isn't settling at night. From diet, to daily routines, sometimes the smallest tweak of daily life can solve the trickiest issues at bedtime.

'What ya' eating there kid?' How food affects sleep

What we eat has more of an effect on how we sleep than you may think.

Our diet plays an important part of sleep for adults as well as children so ditching the junk is beneficial for us all. I mean I love not-so-good-for-me food - don't we all? But it's all about moderation and balance, and it's definitely not about bedtime snacks full of sugar or drinks full of caffeine.

I was helping a parent a few months ago who's 5 year old was a wide-awake party animal every night, even though she had followed my tips to create a calmer time in the hour before bed. There was no issue getting him up to bed, no tears no tantrums or stress - he simply just would not settle and was still wide awake an hour after going to bed.

After a little more investigating (just call me Sherlock,) it came to light that the reward for going up to bed nicely the night before, was a pack of chocolate buttons and a can of pop while watching TV before bed, downstairs.

That nice caffeine and sugar rush was just hitting as their little love headed up to bed. Ouch.

By swapping the crazy snacks for healthier options, it only took 4 nights to work. Of course there was a protest that the chocolate was now a digestive biscuit, and the fizzy pop was warm milk, but it was worth it for the calmer bedtime and happier family life.

Think on your own diet - alcohol before bed might make you feel woozy, but it's actually a stimulant. Think of the food that your kids eat before bed. Do they help themselves to snacks? If so, it's time of day to regulate what's going in before bedtime - especially in that last valuable hour.

*'As dull as it sounds - healthy eating leads
to healthy sleeping, so take a look
at your family diet and make
an adjustment where necessary.'*

Ever heard the phrase 'Never sleep on a full stomach?' It's true - if you want a peaceful night - feed your little loves their evening meal a long time before bed. Anyone who has suffered from heartburn knows just how miserable it is and how sleep is the furthest thing from happening!

Choosing the right foods for the evening meal can avoid tummy aches and tantrums too! Avoid fried or high-fat meals, spicy foods, and fizzy drinks. Ideally your children should be eating a well balanced diet - they're growing and developing and they need essential vitamins and proteins to support this growth. However, as a mum myself, I know kids can be fussy little whatnots, so this is easier said than done. It's really all about the compromise. Have a dedicated 'treat day' instead of regular unhealthy snacks and meals. Your child will thank you for it in the long run (and you'll soon notice a difference in their night-time habits when you ditch the sugary stuff from their diet.)

A better diet for better sleep

For your child's best night's sleep, strive to eat a balanced diet that emphasises fresh fruits, vegetables, whole grains, and low-fat proteins that are rich in B vitamins, like fish, poultry, meat, eggs, and dairy.

B vitamins may also help to regulate melatonin, (a hormone that regulates your sleep cycles!) Food is magic when it comes to sleep see?

Losing weight can lead to better sleep

I'm not about to jump on the diet culture bandwagon here - far from it!

Families that I've worked with, those who follow me on the socials, and those that know me well, know I'm not about dieting or that 'skinny is best,' absolutely no way lovely face. No way at all.

I'm all about embracing our bodies and loving ourselves for who we are and I teach my children that exact same mindset.

We are all different shapes and sizes, and I love that our planet is filled with different shapes and sizes - it's what makes us amazing and diverse human beings. To be unique and wonderful in our own right is wonderful. Having said all this, what matters to me is being healthy. I truly believe we have a responsibility as parents to ensure our children are well looked after and cared for in all areas of development, and this means what food we put into them.

Childhood obesity is an massive problem in the UK. Britain is starting to overtake America in obesity rates, with the latest figures showing that more children in England are classed as obese at the age of 11, than in the US.

The proportion of US children aged 9 to 11 who are obese is 18.5%. The figure for children in their final year of primary school in England is at a record high of 20%. It's pretty worrying, but it's fixable with care and consideration rather than harsh methods and cruel words.

Now I'm not a hippy, green-bean salad feeding mum, like most 8 and 9 year olds, my two would look at me like I was offering poison if I offered a plate of salad and nothing else!

I'll be honest - we have a cheeky Maccy-D's now and then, we also love pizza and sometimes we have 'chip night Friday' from the local chippy, (Chris Fish Bar in Stafford, UK, by the way, do *the* best fish and chips in the world if you're ever in the area!)

Having said all that, I must say we **mainly** eat a well balanced diet and get through a fair amount of fruit and veggies. It's about balance right?

We have a 'treat box' which cereal bars in there, biscuits, maybe even a mini chocolate bar or two at times, but the deal in our house is - if you want a 'not so healthy' snack from the box - there's a fruit-trade first. Same for us grown-ups (in front of the kids at least!)

Eat a piece of fruit - you can have the treat. It works. Honestly - try it.

More often than not, the fruit has filled the craving and they don't want the treat. This idea of course all goes to pot when they are at G&G's house or Nanna and Poppops who offer sweet treats on demand. That's what grandparents are for though hey?

I'm worried my child is overweight - what can I do?

If your child is overweight it can have an effect on sleeping habits, so it's really something to think about. If you are unsure on what the healthy weight range is for your child you can check it out on the NHS website, or chat with your GP.

Eating well is the first step to losing weight, but this doesn't have to mean drastic diets. It can be as simple as switching a few things around and moving around a little more in the day to get within a healthier weight range.

It's important to mention here that you'll need to adjust things in a tactical, calm way without letting on to them that you're worried about their weight. The last thing you want is an upset child that becomes aware or even obsessed over their weight.

Diet culture is crap. I hate it. Social media makes it all ten-times worse and I worry for our pre-teens who see it all online daily. So please, please do it in a calm, no big-deal way to bring them back into a healthy weight range.

It is important to teach children about being healthy, about sugar and fat and about choosing the right foods for their body. Most schools now cover this in the school curriculum. My son who is 8, (Year 3) came home the other day telling us all about saturated fats and healthy food. I was pretty impressed.

Remember - healthy eating doesn't mean ditching all sugary foods and treats altogether - life is too short to not enjoy cake or ice-cream! It's about balance and it's about teaching healthy habits that will take your child through their life.

Exercise not only plays an important part to a healthy body and weight, it also is magical for sleep. There's more on this in the *jump around* chapter of this book which offers lots of ideas on getting kids moving more.

Getting to a healthy weight range for your overweight child can really pay dividends when it comes to getting good sleep. A reduction in body fat, especially around the middle, will make them less likely to struggle with sleep problems like sleep apnea, restlessness, or insomnia. It also makes it less likely that your child will be feeling sleepy and lethargic during the day. Not ideal during the school week.

If you have any major worries about your child's weight, pop along to your GP who will offer support and guidance.

Switch off: Ditching the tech for better sleep!

Guilty as charged - I'm a phone addict. I think the majority of us are and it causes major sleep issues in both adults and children alike.

Kids however - are our responsibility. So although we may create bad habits for ourselves (again - guilty as charged,) it doesn't mean we should allow our children to fall into those awful habits too. I've already touched on this briefly, but tech at bedtime isn't great my friend. It's really bad for us all.

Children and young people spend an increasing amount of time with screens (more than six hours a day according to one US survey) which is quite a huge chunk of their little lives.

Children who use screens this much are also 52% more likely to sleep less than seven hours a night - a significant amount of sleep deprivation with potential consequences for both physical and mental health.

Limiting screen time each week is incredibly important - limiting before bed even more so.

Tethered to tech!

As a society we are tethered to technology, did you know the average adult spends over 10 hours a day looking at some type of electronic screen? Square eyes or what?! Again - I hold my hands up. My daily life mainly involves staring at a screen writing for parenting sites, magazines and answering parenting emails. I do have a cheeky look on ASOS now and again too and find myself losing an hour at a time to social media too! What's worse, is more often than not, some of these 10 hours reported, are while lying in bed scrolling through the screen of our phone.

It's important we don't teach our children these awful habits, and one way is to ditch the tech at bedtime so they follow our lead.

Make the bedroom a no-tech zone!

Getting a good night's sleep is achievable when you take care to not use technology in your bedroom. This means TV's too - so no falling asleep to the TV. It's a big, bad habit that so many parents come to me with. Their children fall asleep beautifully to TV or tech - then when they go through the light sleep phase, they are wide awake!

They need help drifting back off to sleep because they are used to the noise and comfort each night that the tech brings them to sleep. These kind of 'crutches' mean your child relies on something to help them settle rather than learning to fall asleep naturally themselves.

The Blues and your child's circadian rhythm

You know that blue hue coming from your child's phone, TV, and tablet? Did you know it effects their ability to feel satisfied with the sleep they actually get?

The light from the device suppresses melatonin (the magic stuff that induces the sleepy vibe.) This hormone supports your sleep/wake cycle known as the *circadian rhythm,* so, when your cycle is off, you feel less rested. Switching off from any screen time at least 30 minutes before bedtime will lessen this effect on your circadian rhythm and make your child feel a lot better.

Tech Stimulates Your Brain

Depending on what your child watches on TV, or which the game they play on their games console or phone, any of this excitement too close to bedtime will keep your child up longer than you'd like. Tech stimulates the brain so it'll make falling asleep incredibly difficult for them.

It's the same for sending texts, and messages (or older children who check social media.) It stimulates their mind just at the moment they're supposed to be chilling and getting into the sleepy-vibe they need to fall asleep.

Switch off - not silent!

A silent room for sleeping, with no interruptions - is a better sleep space than one that disturbs with phone alerts, phone glow or TV's in the background. So switch off properly, not just silent your child's tech.

Even better, as mentioned before, make the bedroom a 'no tech zone' after a certain time.

I worked with family of tech addicts, who used my 'phone ban box' idea - a simple shoe box in the hallway that all phones went into past 8pm. Even the adults followed the no tech rules.

They switched to old-school alarm clocks and noticed a difference in their sleep as a family in only 3 days!

Of course not all families may want to do this, and not all pre-teens and teenagers will agree to giving up their phone for the night, but think about the rest they will get - the magic sleep needed for the best brain power at school the next day, so maybe ease the idea in twice a week at first and see how it goes.

The struggle to fall asleep is real, it can cause upset and stress and worry for so many parents, but making small changes can make a huge difference.

Sometimes, the struggle to fall asleep can be caused by anxiety or night fears. Head over to the *Anxious child* or the next chapter; *Things that Go Bump in the night* for more on that.

Chapter Four
Things that go bump in the night: Dealing with night fears, nightmares and night-terrors in a cool and calm way.

Night terrors, nightmares and night fears are all pretty common in young children and one of the biggest cause of sleep issues for families.

Sadly, all children will have a night terror or nightmare at some point during their life. It's a horrid, scary and worrying thing to go through for both parent and child but it's more common than you think. Most children grow out of them, and they don't cause any long-term psychological harm, so try not to worry if your child is going through them at the moment.

Why is my child having night mares?

If your child has suddenly started waking in the night because of night terrors, nightmares, or night fears, there are a number of reasons why this may be happening.

From a house move, to a new sibling to even starting a new school year - there are all kinds of reasons your sound sleeper has joined *The Wide Awake Kids Club* due to nightmares and fears.

Before we take a look at my tips for dealing with these issues, let's look at the difference between a nightmare and a night terror as the two are actually different things.

What's the difference between a night terror and nightmare?

Night Terrors: A night terror, also known as a *sleep terror,* predominantly affects young children, and causes feelings of terror or dread. A night terror typically occurs in the first half-hour, to an hour of sleep.

Though night terrors can be alarming for parents who witness them, they're not usually cause for concern or a sign of a deeper medical issue, so try not to worry.

Children who have night terrors usually shout out or scream in their sleep, sit or stand up, and have a look of fear on their face. They will usually sweat, breathe fast and have a rapid heart rate too.

What causes night terrors?

- Night terrors are caused by over-arousal of the central nervous system during sleep. This may happen because the central nervous system which regulates sleep and waking brain activity, is still maturing.

- Some children may even inherit a tendency for this over-arousal (about 80% who have night terrors have a family member who also has experienced them or sleepwalking!)

- Night terrors are most commonly triggered by being overtired, so it's back to them favourite phrase *routine is the magic key!* Getting a better bedtime routine and sleep habits, in turn, helps an overtired child.

- Sometimes sleeping in a new bed or being away from home can trigger a night terror.

- New changes can sometime start night terrors or nightmares such as a house move, new school, new class or a new sibling arrival.

- Illness/fever can also cause night terrors.

What can I do to help?

The best possible way to handle night terrors is to comfort and reassure your child and snuggle them back down in their own bed. It's tempting to invite your child into your own bed, but it's really important to keep them in *their own* bed so they don't associate the bad dream with their bedroom.

A child who is used to sleeping all night in their own bed may suddenly not want to sleep there anymore, as they associate the 'bad experience' with their room and a happier experience in with you in your bed.

Reassure them in their own bed, sit with them for a while and pop on a night-light until they are calm. Stay with your child in their own room until they are feeling more relaxed and their breathing is settled.

Nightmares: A nightmare is an bad dream that usually causes upset and fear, and are pretty common in young children. Unlike night terrors, a nightmare usually occurs sometime after 1-2 hours of sleep.

If your child has had a nightmare they will usually find it hard to get back to sleep. They usually will be very distressed and upset, and in extreme cases find settling back to sleep after their first one through worry of the nightmare returning.

When nightmares become more frequent or occur on a regular basis, it may be a sign of stress in your child's life or environment. Don't panic! This doesn't necessarily mean something terrible and traumatic, it can be something as simple as changing teachers at school, moving house, starting a new school or a new sibling arrival.

What causes night terrors?

- Eating late at night is a big contributor to nightmares. (Eating before bed triggers an increase in the body's metabolism and brain activity.)

- Loss: The of a relative or even family pet can trigger nightmares, as can family separations. If you feel that these may be the cause of your child's bad dreams, it's important to address the issues in the day by talking, drawing, reading and reassuring them through the difficult time.

- Frightening stories/TV shows: Something not so scary to us grown-ups, can be really frightening for children, so have a think about what your little ones are watching or reading/looking at during the day. Nightmares can often happen after reading or watching frightening things before bed, so while I'd not like to discourage bedtime stories, or reading at bedtime, I'd advise steering clear of frightening books (older children) or perhaps avoid monster stories for younger children if they have started to have nightmares.

- Over-tiredness: Nightmares are most commonly triggered by being overtired, so, again, it's the old *routine is the magic key* - phrase of mine! Get a good bedtime routine in place to ensure they are getting top quality sleep, and enough hours each night.

- New changes can sometime start night terrors or nightmares such as a house move, new school or new baby.

- Sometimes sleeping in a new bed, new sheets/bedding or being away from home can trigger a nightmare.

What can I do to help?

If you have suffered a nightmare yourself, you will possibly remember the feelings of worry and fear after. Sometimes bad dreams seem very real and can be terribly upsetting and leave you in a bit of a daze thinking about them and repeating them in your head.

Like night terrors, the best possible way to handle night terrors is to cuddle and reassure your child and snuggle them back down in their bed. Make them feel safe again and talk through the dream with them if they can remember it. Reassure them that although it seems very real, our brains are incredibly smart and can conjure up all kinds of things that can frighten us and are just not real.

Stay with your little one until they are calm and their breathing is settled. As mentioned before, it's really important to let them get back to sleep themselves, so don't be tempted to put them into your bed and cuddle them to sleep, even if it seems the easiest option at the time, it'll make their own bed seem frightening and your bed the safer option.

During the day, read books or chat about having bad dreams to reassure your child these are a normal thing and nothing to worry about. Tell them that you sometimes have bad dreams too.

Invest in a low light, torch or nightlight to reassure and help with any fears of the dark that often come with nightmares. A few drops of lavender oil in their bath before bedtime is a lovely way of getting your them to feel calmer and ready for bed, or mix some lavender oil with water to spray on bed sheets or pillows before bed.

As a mum myself, who has been up in the night many times with my two and their nightmares, fears and sometimes night terrors, I understand how distressing it is for you as a parent, but try not to worry and always remain calm.

Remember that nightmares and night terrors are normal, and they will pass and are part of childhood.

Night fears: Monsters, ghosts and other stories

It's a common bedtime issue, and one that should always be taken seriously. The things that go bump in the night. I know they're not real, and you know they're not real, but your child's fears are very real *to them*.

From monsters under the bed, to ghostly drapes at the windows, your child's fear is very real to them and can cause panic, tears and a lack of bedtime enthusiasm night after night. It can often be something as simple as the dark itself. The key to solving bedtime fears is to *pinpoint what the fear is.*

Fears cause anxiety, and anxiety means that little imaginative brain is ticking away and not allowing sleep to come at all, night after night. This in turn causes over tiredness and if you've read the previous chapters, you'll know this is a major cause of sleepless nights.

'Monsters are scary.

Always check the cupboards and under the bed.

Yea, I know there's no monsters there - but your

child's fear is very real to them!'

To figure out exactly what is causing the anxiety, chat with your child during the day.

Painting, drawing, talking, even letting them write it in a thought diary, will help you to understand the worries they have at bedtime and address the issue together.

If your child is scared of monsters, ghosts and witches: Simply saying *'there's no such thing as monsters'* won't work. Getting annoyed doesn't help either, so keep your cool and listen to what they have to say.

Always check the cupboards and under the bed. Yea, I know there's no monsters there - but your child's fear is very real to them. By checking, it's not saying you *believe* there is a monster there, it's simply reassuring your child that you are listening to them and helping them to settle.

Get them to check with you if they will. Give them a torch to shine under the bed and in the cupboards, then blitz the air with your very own monster spray!

Talk about monsters and witches and ghosts - where did their ideas of these things come from? Maybe they read something in a book or something on TV, or maybe someone at school has told them scary stories. My little girl was told a silly story at school by another child about a ghostly figure that would appear in the mirror or hide under the bed to get you if you said a certain thing. She was absolutely terrified to go to bed or look in a mirror through fear that this character would appear.

We talked it all through as a silly, made-up story, that was simply designed to scare others. Then we looked in the mirror together and said the thing she was told, and we checked under her bed. I'm pleased to report no scary figure appeared and we both survived to tell the tale.

I explained how just like spooky movies or halloween, none of it is real, it just makes us feel scared. I also reminded her that scared can sometimes be fun too, like at Halloween when we dress up as scary as can be.

Monster sprays and worry toys. If things are particularly tough, sometimes objects can help like worry dolls or monster sprays.

Monster spray is so easy to make or you can buy lavender sprays and put a homemade 'monster spray' label on it yourself. To make your own, simply mix water with fresh lavender or lavender oil drops for a soothing spritz in the air. This ghost fighting, monster bashing, mind calming spray, will help calm even grown-ups exhausted minds, so spray your own pillows too! It's lush.

Worry dolls are pretty cool too. There are a few available to buy (I love the Sorgonfresser dolls) or, if you're a wiz on a sewing machine like my mate Ceri, you could even make your own!

You can put a note into the pocket or mouth of these cuddly toys, and it takes the worry away. They're great fun (but parents - you kinda have to remember to take the worry note away here for it to work, so if you are a really crap tooth fairy, you might want to give this idea a miss!)

If your child is scared of the dark: Some sleep experts say that sleeping in total darkness is best, and while I agree for young babies and toddlers this works well, as children grow, their imaginations begin to go wild and they often develop a fear of the dark. It really isn't anything to worry about, but is something that needs dealing with in an understanding and caring way.

Night lights: Investing in a night light can often be the simple answer for *Wide Awake Kids Club* members that struggle to settle. A low light, bed light or even wall plug-in night light, can often be enough to offer that soft glow of reassurance in the dark.

Point to remember here: In spring ,when the clock changes occur, remember to pop the light on when they go to bed in the light! I have made this mistake many times, forgetting to switch it on as it is still light in the evenings, only to hear upset shrieks from a little one that has woken to find the room pitch black now it's later in the evening! Oops.

Projector lamps are a pretty cool, inexpensive way, of helping a 'dark fear' vanish. There are plenty available to buy from only a few pounds. These nights lights come in all kinds of designs, from starry skies projected across the ceiling, to dancing unicorns. These style night-lights are often so soothing, they lull even the widest awake child to sleep in a gentle, calming way.

Walks in the dark: Encourage outings in the dark such as winter walks in the early evening with torches, camping out in summer, or even going to the cinema together as a family, these adventures can help with fears of the dark.

Glow in the dark toys: Age seven, my Nanna bought me a *glo-worm* and I loved it! That gentle glow, under the bed covers ,just gave me the extra comfort I needed at night to drift off. There are so many light-up toys available now (too many to mention,) so have a look around and see if any interest your child. Remember to buy toys only from reputable outlets and always look for the CE symbol.

If your child is scared of shapes and shadows in their bedroom: Bedrooms in the day are often fun places filled with toys and games and fun times. At night the shadows created by lights and toys, can often worry children and get the imagination running wild. Anyone who's seen *Monsters inc.* will know what I mean.

Look around your child's room. Are there any particular spots of the room that seem to be darker or cause more fear at night than others? Chat with your little one about the areas that worry them and think about rearranging the room a little bit, to create a safer, happier space.

Using a night-light might reassure them, or fairy lights hung safely out of reach can create a calmer and cosier feel to the room.

If you're feeling super energetic and creative and the fears of the room are really causing issues, consider a room change or a redecoration! Get your child involved in the planning and decorating.

Make their bedroom a 'safe space' for them to relax in at the end of the day. This is often a good idea with older children who have 'outgrown' their younger bedroom.

My daughter and son both recently had a surprise room upgrade and love it so much they are often up in their rooms writing and painting. Bedtimes are rarely an issue as they love their rooms so much! What's ace is it didn't cost much to upgrade both rooms at all. Just lick of paint, some wall stickers, new duvet cover and change around, made their rooms look totally different.

Whatever fears your child might have at night, always deal with the wake-ups and upsets in a calm way.

As a mum myself, I do understand how hard it is to be understanding and chilled at 3am, but by being understanding and kind - you'll be back to bed much faster and happier than if you all lose your cool.

Night fears are usually something that children grow out of, so try not to worry. Having said this, if you do have any real concerns, and your child is showing quite worrying signs of distress when it comes to the dark, or their night fears night after night, talk to your GP.

Chapter Five
Ch, ch, ch, changes - Getting back into good sleep habits after school holidays and clock changes!

There are so many ch, ch, ch, changes (sorry! Huge Bowie fan here,) that can disrupt a usual happy sleeper and make them become fully fledged *Wide Awake kids Club* members.

Two of the biggest changes to effect a usually brilliant sleeper, are the clock changes and the school holidays.

In the UK, the clocks go forward an hour in Spring, and back an hour in Winter and can cause chaos even with that little hour of change.

The glorious school holidays bring their own bedtime changes and can have the happy sleeper, turn in to a *midnight gang member* in no time at all though over-tiredness and lack of routine to their days.

I love school holidays. Don't we all? We all fall into holiday habits when we go away, you know the thing, the late nights and lazy mornings, and while these are wonderful and O.K for a week or two, they can cause major issues on the return to school.

Not only do they stop decent bedtime hours, but the getting up for school in the mornings can be a total nightmare and not something you want on a Monday morning!

So how do we ensure these ch, ch, ch changes (sorry) don't make everything go wrong that we've previously worked hard to achieve?

School holidays

Preparation is key: It takes about a week to get back into the old school routine, so in the long school holidays, start gradually moving your child's bedtime earlier in 15-minute or 30-minute increments each night until you are back to their regular bedtime.

Do the same with their morning wake-ups. So, if you've been lucky enough to have some lazy starts during the school holidays - get them back into their earlier mornings so the back-to-school early starts, aren't a complete nightmare and shock to everyone.

Use a bedtime clock: As mentioned in previous chapters, a bedtime clock is not only ideal for your midnight gang member or early riser - it is great for getting kids back into the school sleep routine. It's also great for pre-teens, who may like to hit snooze on a regular alarm clock in favour of a lie-in. (The bedtime clocks don't have snooze functions!)

Stick to the routine at weekends: Once you've worked hard to create good sleep habits, it can be so easy to ruin them by letting it all go at the weekend. Sticking to a good sleep schedule 24-7, will benefit your child and you, so avoid the super-late weekend nights in favour of maybe just the extra half-hour for younger children, and maybe an hour for older ones.

The daily routine while on holiday

'In the school holidays or while away on holiday, it is easy to

fall out of routine, Instead of ditching the routine altogether

- stick to it loosely.'

If the school summer holidays are leading to later bedtimes - don't worry! The holidays are for fun times, but you can still keep a routine in place. Stick to the same bedtime routine but just increase the stay-up time! My two usually go to bed at 7pm in term time, but in the glorious summer holiday evenings, they play out in the garden for longer and head to bed a little later. The routine is still in place - it's just a little later rather than a different time each night.

Remember, a week before the back-to-normality returns, and the routine of school comes back, start decreasing the holiday 'stay-up time' by 15 minutes a night, until you are back to their regular bedtime and ready and refreshed for back to school days.

Jet lag and the wide-awake kid

I've been lucky enough to travel to far-off places in my time, and a few times with the little loves in tow. One thing I don't love about travelling is jet lag.

For adults, jet lag sucks, but what's worse is helping kids get into the vibe of a new time zone. Nobody wants to start their holiday cranky! With this in mind - there's a few things you can try to make jet-lag a little lighter.

Shift the body clock before you travel: Lots of my travelling parent buddies, have told me they find travelling easier when they shift their body clocks a few days before travel to prepare in advance. Children's circadian rhythms generally catch up with them naturally after 3 or 4 days, so it's not essential to do this before you travel, but could make it easier for younger little loves.

Sometimes, shifting your child's bedtime by a couple of hours toward the destination time-zone a few days before your travel can really help.

Get into the time zone at the airport: Set your clocks to the time of your destination so you feel like you're already on that time zone. By doing this before you arrive, you are tricking yours and your child's body into the new time zone.

If it's night-time in the place you're landing, but daytime on the plane - try and encourage a good few hours sleep on the journey there to get the body thinking it's bedtime. With children this can be easier said than done - so let them settle first watching a movie in exchange for a sleep later. With this in mind, let them travel in comfortable clothes and have their favourite sleep-comfort handy so it puts them in the sleep zone frame of mind.

Keep hydrated: Travelling dehydrates us quickly - so keep your little loves topped up, even if this means frequent bathroom visits on the plane. I know, I know - bathroom visits on an aircraft with kids isn't fun, but you'll all feel better for keeping hydrated!

Dehydration can add to that woozy jet-lag feeling when we land in the new time-zone, so by keeping hydrated you're all less likely to feel awful and more able to enjoy your holiday right away.

Get some sunshine: While it's important to be sun-safe (don't forget to pile on the sun-cream,) if you are arriving at what would be your little ones bedtime, get out in the sunshine and soak up the rays. Sunlight helps your body and brain make sense of the new time zone and resets your inner clock, so try and keep them awake as long as possible into the new time-zone.

On a recent trip to New York, my little boy was falling asleep into his burger in our fave diner (Tick Tock diner, 481 8th Avenue - corner of 34th Street if you're asking!)

It was way past his bedtime in the UK, but in NYC it was early afternoon!
A few milkshakes and funny stories later - he was soon wide awake and ready for an adventure before an early bedtime for us all.

Sleep aids for jet-lag: You may find your child wide-awake during the first few nights on your holiday or indeed on their return home while trying to adjust - this doesn't mean reaching for quick fix solutions is a good idea.

While American (adults) swear by melatonin to help with their time-difference adjustment, in the UK this isn't available without prescription and really isn't advisable for children who have not been prescribed it for ongoing sleep or medical issues.

In a recent Guardian article on *Too many children being prescribed melatonin to aid sleep,*' a Royal Pharmaceutical Society spokesperson, Lesley McArthur, said: 'I'd be concerned about people buying melatonin online. It's a prescription-only medicine and you can't be certain that what you are buying is the real thing.'

so lovely faces, instead of reaching for medication, or sleep aids, stick with routine, consistency and just go with it for a bit. Things will get back to normal in time when the body clock adjusts, so be cool.

Sleeping in the heat - how to help your child sleep on holiday and keep their cool!

In the glorious summer months or while on holiday, sleep can often become disrupted due to the heat or a change in routine. A lack of sleep added to hot summer days can result in a grumpy child and unhappy parents which isn't a fun way to spend the summer at all!

Fan-tastic sleep! It's worth investing in a fan for the summer months as they can really make a difference to hot, muggy bedrooms.

By circulating the air in your child's room, you're keeping them from the risk of overheating, waking and thus helping them get a good nights sleep.

It's important to note here that if you're using a fan to be safe. Ensure it is out of younger children's reach (including wires) and that it's not pointed directly at their bed.

Too hot to sleep? Hot sticky nights cause disrupted sleep for many adults who can re-adjust their bedclothes or pyjamas to get comfy! Children, especially younger ones, rely on us to keep them comfortable and cool at night, so think comfort when putting your child to bed in hot weather.

Less is best so rather than pyjamas - let them sleep in underwear to avoid over-heating. Avoid quilts too until the cooler weather returns opting for sheets instead.

If you want to have a window open and are at home - please consider using safety locks. If you're lucky enough to have safety windows that open a small amount and are lockable, then these are even better. Don't be tempted to leave regular, (non-safety) windows open wide. It's really not worth the risk and I have heard some terrible stories over the years working with families. Some too tragic to share with you here.

Leave bedroom doors open, and use a fan (as mentioned above,) to circulate the air in their room - this often keeps the whole home cool in warmer months.

Dealing with clock changes

Springtime - Spring forward into a happy bedtime: When we put the clocks forward it means an hours less sleep for us (I know, I know,) but it also means an hour less for your child too.

You can avoid problems, strops and grumpiness that early-waking brings, by getting your child ready about a week before the clock changes.

Simply change bedtimes to 10-15 minutes earlier each night for seven nights. This simple tip can really help make the transition smoother and the clock change tick tock along nicely. If you're reading this with less than seven nights to prepare - don't worry, start as soon as you can, even a couple of nights before the clock-change can really help.

With older children, if you are not already using one, use the sleep clock as mentioned in previous chapters, as these are fantastic for letting kids know when it is O.K to get up out of bed and come to you.

You may need to pop them back to bed for a few mornings in the first few days of a clock-change until they've settled into the new time.

If they are wide-awake only half an hour before the clock is due to change into the sunshine, reading books in bed is fine! I encourage this for early wakers as it gets them into a little routine of waking gently, and waiting until the right get-up time. My two, especially in lighter mornings, often wake at 6 am on school mornings but will 'read' until the 'sunshine' appears on their bedtime clock at 6.30am. On weekends - they don't come down before 8am and read in bed happily.

Autumn time - Fall back into better bedtimes: This means an extra hour of glorious sleep for most people! For us parents – not so lucky.

In the autumn - simply reverse the springtime clock change tips above.

Whereas before, in Springtime you may need black-out blinds or curtains to help sleep in the lighter evenings, you may find the new winter times are on your side. Children often sleep better in the winter because of our dark mornings and earlier dark nights.

As mentioned in the Springtime tips, with older children, if you are not already using one – use a sleep clock. These clocks are fantastic and really help them to know when it is O.K to get up out of bed and get you. Simply change the clock at bedtime - and explain to your child that if they wake early, they must wait for the sunshine.

Finally, the the week after clock changes you may find your child is unsettled. Try not to worry, they'll soon settle once they get into the new time. By sticking to your usual daily routine, and a great, regular, bedtime routine you'll soon have a happy sleeper again.

Whatever ch, ch, ch ,changes occur during your child's daily life - the sooner you get back to routine and stick with it, you'll all be back to better sleep in no time at all.

Chapter Six
Anxiety and the sleep deprived: Tips for calming and coping with an anxious child

Just like us grown-ups, children can feel worried and anxious at times too. From as young as 8 months old, a child can show anxiety in the form of *separation anxiety*. This anxiety is where little ones they become clingy and really upset when separated from their parents. (There's a whole post on coping with that over on my website *www.childcareisfun.co.uk* if you have younger ones!) This anxiety is a totally normal stage of development and they grow it of it, usually around 3 years old.

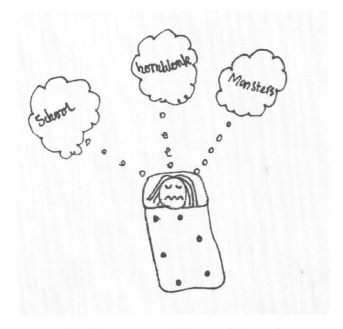

'Just like us grown-ups, children can feel worried

and anxious at times too.'

Other worries and anxieties in childhood include phobias or fears. This often starts in the pre-school years and can include fears of animals, insects, storms, heights, water, blood, and the dark. These fears usually go away gradually on their own.

My daughter had a very strange fear - the sound of sticky-tape being pulled from the roll, and my son hated the sound of the lawnmower. My daughter now gets through sticky-tape with her crafting activities like it's going out of fashion, and my son would actually cut the grass with the lawnmower now if we let him!

In older children anxiety can occur when going to a new school, moving home or before tests and exams. They could be anxious due to family arguments, worries about family members who are unwell, or they may have been through a traumatic experience.

The key, during all of these periods of anxiety is to offer reassurance, guidance and support and to always encourage your child to talk about how they feel.

How do I know if my child is anxious?

Children often struggle to explain their feelings, so it's important to look out for symptoms of worry and anxiety which can include;

- Feeling irritable, tearful or clingy
- Difficulties in sleeping or getting off to sleep
- Suddenly start wetting the bed
- Nightmares or night terrors

Older children may show different symptoms such as;

- Not wanting to try new things or lack confidence
- Seem unable to face simple, everyday challenges
- May have negative thoughts going around their head, or feel like bad things might happen
- Start avoiding friends and stop talking to family
- Have a lack of concentration
- Have problems with sleeping
- A change in appetite
- May be prone to bursts of anger

How to help your anxious child

It's worrying when you see your child distressed and showing signs of anxiety, and this anxiety can often play a big part in the ability to fall asleep and stay asleep, but the key to helping them through these episodes, is to be calm and consistent.

Talk, talk, and talk some more: Talking is incredibly important - so chat with your child about their worries or any concerns they may have. Using my *'three awesomes and one rubbish'* technique at bedtime (as featured in the previous chapter,) is a great way of finding out anything that is worrying them.

Don't avoid anxiety triggers: Avoiding triggers won't help your child learn to cope in the long run, and remember - not all triggers can be avoided. In fact, though avoidance might help children feel better in the short-term, it can amplify the fears over time. Instead, help your child to learn how to tolerate their feelings of anxiety develop coping strategies together to manage it. You'll help them in the long-term if you do this.

Don't let them isolate themselves: It's often the case that an anxious child wants to be alone, but over time this can make matters worse.

If your child repeatedly declines play-date invites or refuses to try a new after-school activity - the temptation may be to say 'it's OK don't go if you are worried.' However, this won't help your child long-term. It is pretty much saying that if you worry about something, it means you can't do it.

Instead, offer a solution to the concern they have about going on the pay date, or attending the activity, and encourage them to go. More often than not - they will have a wonderful time and realise the worries they had were unfounded.

Routine is the magic key: Oh I know - I've said it again, but honestly, just like sleep, a good routine can help anxiety, because regular activity, regular socialising and regular bedtimes all help your child to feel comforted with things that they know and trust and this helps them to feel less anxious.

Get moving more! A regular exercise routine can help to reduce anxiety, in fact just five minutes of exercise can trigger anti-anxiety responses in the body. Read more in my exercise chapter where there's lots of lovely tips from qualified PT *Sean Dawson* on getting kids moving more, and how exercise is beneficial for sleep.

Find books about worries: Either looking at books together or letting them read books about the things that worry them can really help. Fears of the dark, worrying about a potential hospital visit or even the loss of a loved one are all common topics covered in children books.

Preparation is key! If you know a big change is coming such as a house move, or new school year and know your child is prone to anxiety - prepare them in advance to any big event. Mark the date on a calendar and look forward to the event rather than worry about it.

Talk about everything that will happen, plan ahead, give them tasks to help towards the date, so , for example, if you're moving house - get them to help by packing up there room. Talk all the time and get them to express any concerns or worries they have about the event.

Talk about how adults get anxiety too! Make it normal - there's nothing worse than feeling like you're the only one going through something, and anxiety can be very scary for a child.

Try some calming techniques: Practice simple relaxation techniques with your child, such as taking three deep, slow breaths, breathing in for a count of three and out for three. You'll find more relaxation techniques in my Yoga and Meditation chapter. There'a a really special 'chocolate meditation' plan by Claudia that is particularly wonderful for anxious kids.

Sometimes a relaxing music download is helpful for children who are really struggling to settle. There are lots of meditation podcasts, tracks and playlists on iTunes and Deezer.

Try a comforter! If your child has a hard time separating from you at bedtime, try a transitional object. This is a special item that helps your child feel comforted.

It could be a soft toy or a blanket, or even a handkerchief sprayed with some of your aftershave or perfume. (I have a popular 'back-to-school hanky' post on my facebook page *'Childcare is Fun'* that is popular with new starters. Often taking a small hanky sprayed with perfume or aftershave - really helps them feel reassured on the first days of school!)

Remember - there really is no age limit when it comes to comforters at bedtime. Age 44 I still sleep with a teddy bear (his name is Blue and he is soft and lovely) and I don't care who knows it!

Make a worry book or box: Invest in a journal or make a worry box where your child can write their worries down.

Writing about worries helps children learn to vent their anxious feelings and often makes them feel so much better. This is particularly helpful for a child who is reluctant to talk about their worries. Get an old tissue box or shoe box - cut a small, rectangular hole like a postbox shape, and decorate it. Leave it somewhere the whole family can use it! Or get a nice plain notebook or journal where anyone can write down their thoughts, feelings or worries.

You can then have a daily or weekly family 'worry meeting' where you go through the box or book and talk about what's worrying you. (Obviously us grown-ups have quite big worries sometimes that we don't want to put onto our little ones - so go steady with the worries you share! Keep it simple like 'I forgot to pay a parking fine and can't find the ticket' or something like that?)

Throwing our worries away! A fun and effective anxiety-basher, is to write down a feeling or thought and then crumple or tear the paper and throw it away. This technique has helped lots of children I've worked with to feel like the worry has *physically* been taken away.

Use a worry toy: I've mentioned these in a previous chapter already, but worry dolls are pretty cool. There are a few available to buy or you could even make your own.

You can put a note with your worry on, into the pocket or mouth of these cuddly toys, and it takes the worry away. They're great fun (but again, parents - you kinda have to remember to take the worry note away here, so if you are a really crap tooth fairy, you might want to give this idea a miss!)

Shhh that thought! Teach your child how to shush their worrying thoughts by verbally telling them to be quiet! (*Their worrying thoughts - not your child!*) When intrusive thoughts overwhelm children, they go into fight-or-flight mode, the heart can start to race, they can feel overwhelmed and their emotions can snowball, so help them to stop the thoughts progressing by shushing them. Tell them to say (out loud) *"NO! THAT ISN'T REAL OR TRUE!"* when an intrusive worry comes into their head. This technique interrupts the anxious thought cycle and can stop anxiety in it's tracks. Older children might feel silly doing this, so encourage them to push the thoughts away by deleting them as if they were on their laptop. Delete, delete, delete, and into the TRASH BIN.

Make a chill kit! One of my favourites is to fill a box with relaxing activities and comforting things chosen by your child and have it in their bedroom. This include relaxing music on a music player, calming books, lavender spray, fidget spinners, stress balls, snow globe, music box, small cuts of ribbons and different textured fabrics to feel, or a comforter.

Keep this box by the bed for times of anxiety. Let them have the box in bed and unwind using the chill kit in peace for half an hour. Then go up to settle them for the night. You'll often find they are already asleep!

Practice Relaxation Strategies Children need to learn how to regulate both their emotional and physical responses (they become intertwined) when they go into fight-or-flight mode. This is where Meditation and Yoga can really help bedtime anxiety battles! Check out my *Hippy kids* chapter for lots of lovely tips from Yoga queen (and generally lovely lady,) Claudia Brown!

Finally, remember, all children are different and what works well for one child might not work for another, so work together to understand and manage symptoms of their anxiety. Don't expect a quick fix - finding ways to cope with triggers takes time and practice so work your way through the ideas and suggestions above to see what works best for you and your child.

When should we get extra help?

Anxiety is a real worry and stress for both parents and children, but it is something that is common and often goes away with time, patience and trying different techniques.

Having said this, if your child's anxiety is severe, persists and interferes with their everyday life, it's a good idea to get some help, so make an appointment with your GP.

If your child's anxiety is affecting their school life too, chat with their teacher to make them aware of what is going on - they often have support in school and recourses available to you and your child.

There are plenty of online resources to help parents dealing with childhood anxiety such as *Young Minds*. Details of these organisations are at the back of this book in the reference section.

Chapter Seven
Jump around! Jump around! Jump-up, jump-up and…(Get some sleep!) How exercise creates better sleep

I'll admit to sometimes being one of those fitness bore-offs on Instagram - I love training, and I love running. I don't do it to loose weight though (or to get beach body ready,) I actually do it to get strong, fit and to keep my mind happy.

Without wanting to sound like some fitness-guru, (I'm far from one of those) there are so many health benefits that exercise has on our lives, but did you know that exercise can provide excellent benefits for your sleep too? True story.

Research indicates that exercise, in particular, regular exercise, that's part of a consistent routine - can help boost sleep duration, in addition to sleep quality. Now that's something to definitely encourage if your little one is a frequent member of the *midnight gang!*

I had a chat with qualified Personal Trainer *Sean Dawson*, about how to get kids moving more, and how exercise benefits sleep.

Hello Sean! Please share with the lovely reader, your background and experiences when it comes to exercise.

Hello! I've been studying and working within the health and fitness industry since 2004.

After studying Sports Science at both College and University, I followed my passion to help others improve their health and fitness, and achieve goals they thought were never possible when going at it alone. People often ask me what my dream job is, and I can confidently reply, 'this is!'

I truly believe in the ancient saying, *'Choose a job you love, and you will never have to work a day in your life.'* That's where I feel I am right about now.

That's pretty cool Sean - so you know what you're talking about when it comes to keeping healthy and fit? Tell us Sean, what are the benefits of doing regular exercise for healthier sleep?

Exercise can improve sleep in so many ways. It can improve sleep quality by spending more time in *deep sleep*, increase sleep duration due to the amount of energy used in physical activity (leaving us more tired and needing the rest,) and reduce stress and anxiety which will help us fall asleep faster!

It also helps with insomnia and other sleep disorders as exercise can be a natural therapy.

Let's face it Sean, not all kids love to to move. With tech taking over this modern world, how can we encourage a reluctant child to give exercise a go?

You've got to start with small steps and find something they enjoy.

If a child is reluctant, it's most likely because they don't enjoy doing what is being offered. So you need to find ways of getting them exercising in a way they find fun and will want to keep doing.

Think about what your child likes; Do they enjoy the outdoors (cycling, walking, playground activities?) Do they perhaps enjoy the social aspect of playing with friends or being involved within team sports? Maybe they have a passion to excel in an individual activity such as tennis, swimming, golf etc? Or you could simply start by getting them more active by walking or cycling more often to places, instead of taking the car.

Once you've found something they really enjoy, introduce 15 minutes of this new activity to their week. Swap 15 minutes of sedentary activities (watching TV, or playing computer games,)for the new activity and put it on the calendar so you're all committed to it as a family.

After two weeks, introduce another 15 minute block, or even a new activity, but again, replace this extra time your child usually spends inactive.

Great tips Sean! Are there certain child-friendly exercises, sports or activities that you'd suggest?

Rather than focusing on one particular sport - prioritise finding an activity which your child enjoys. If you choose something they don't enjoy, they will be more reluctant to do it.

Exercise can be as simple as walking to school, playing in the playground, and climbing trees. Or it can be something more structured like gymnastics, dancing, or martial arts.

Find something they enjoy, whether that be as a team, with friends or family, or just on their own, and support them through it.

'Rather than focusing on one particular sport - prioritise finding an activity that your child enjoys. If you choose something they don't enjoy, they will be more reluctant to do it. Exercise can be as simple as walking to school, playing in the playground!'

Not all parents have funds to support after-school sports. Do you have any tips for simple-to-follow exercise sessions children can do in their front room or back yard?

I think I'm showing my age here, but I truly believe in going *old school* with things like playing tag, climbing trees, swings climbing frames and trampolines.

Indoor activities can include dance mats, physical games like Twister, or setting challenges such as 'who can hold the longest plank?' Or seeing how many push-ups or sit-ups they can do. Turn it into a fun game as a family - kids love competition! This in turn becomes family quality time spent with your children and benefits your own health too.

I love those ideas - I'm quite competitive myself and love the idea of a plank or sit-up challenge!

Sean, we hear all the time as adults how often we should exercise, but how often (ideally) should children get moving?

The NHS guidelines for children (5-18-years) to maintain a *basic level of health and fitness* is at least 60 minutes of moderate to vigorous physical activity every day.

Three days a week - these activities should involve exercises for strong muscles and bones, such as swinging on playground equipment, impact activities such as hopping, skipping, dancing, and sports such as gymnastics, rugby, and martial arts.

At least 60 minutes sounds like a lot, but remember, this can be anything from walking the dog, running in the playground, playing on the trampoline in the garden, dancing at the school disco, cycling to visit grandparents instead of driving, or taking the stairs instead of escalators.

My advice is, if your child is nowhere near these guidelines - don't panic and overdo it all at once. Instead, increase their physical activity by 15 minutes each week, until they are hitting these guidelines. Small steps over 6-12 months will lead to a much more sustainable and healthier lifestyle.

Remember finding this time can be as simple as taking away 15 minutes of sedentary activities that your child usually has.

Wow Sean! That's quite a lot of activity our kids need each day - I had no idea it was that much!

Let's be honest though - often children just love tech-time over *getting out there* moving. So, with this in mind - are there any child-friendly exercise or fitness apps or online resources you'd recommend?

There are a couple of apps to get your children moving more such as '*The 7-Minute Workout for Kids.*' It's made up of exercises using their own bodyweight so there's no need for any equipment.

In this 7 minutes, there are brief moments of intense exercise followed by short rest periods to recover. What's great is these seven minute workouts can slot in to every child's daily routine.

Another app I'd recommend is called *'Yoga For Kids Daily Fitness.'* Not only will this increase physical strength but also mental strength as well.

And lastly, if your children love tech, I'd recommend wristband fitness-trackers for them. It's another fun way to get children active. The fitness bands track and reward steps, active minutes and sleep.

Thanks Sean! These tips are fantastic, and as soon as I've finished writing this paragraph - I'm off to order some fitness trackers for my two!

I'd also like to mention a pretty cool YouTube channel called *Cosmic Kids Yoga* - it's perfect for before bedtime!

If you are feeling a little exhausted after all the fitness chat, go grab a cuppa and get ready for a nice chill-out vibe the next chapter has to offer.

In this next chapter I'll be chatting all things Yoga and meditation and the benefits it has for sleep, with Yoga instructor (Queen) *Claudia Brown.*

Claudia shares with me her tips and experiences and shares with you the magic that yoga can do for your child's sleep!

Chapter Eight
The Hippy Kids Club - How Yoga and Meditation can aid sleep

I think sometimes Yoga, and meditation, is seen as a bit of a hippy, non-sensical thing for those who have never tried it. I'll be totally honest, that was me before meeting Claudia about a year ago.

Now? Well, I'm no yoga master, and I'm still learning, but woah - has my attitude to yoga and meditation changed!

My sleep is better, my mental health better, and I'm getting super bendy and less achey. What's even more awesome is my little ones love it too and it gets them proper-chilled and in the bedtime mind-frame when we practice together before bed.

Yoga, for those that don't know, is a mind and body practice with a 5,000-year history in ancient Indian philosophy. Various styles of yoga combine physical postures, breathing techniques, and meditation or relaxation.

Claudia Brown is a Yoga teacher based in Stafford (but is a proud Cumbrian,) she also happens to be my Yoga Queen of Awesome. I chatted to her about all things Yoga, Meditation and the benefits it can have for children struggling with sleep issues.

Namaste! Tell us about you Claudia - what's your background, qualifications and experiences when it comes to Yoga and Meditation?

Namaste my little pal!

I'm a yoga teacher and I offer classes, private tuition and luxury day yoga retreats.

I work with corporate clients such as iProspect, Risual, Staffordshire Police and Staffordshire Women's Aid. I did my initial Yoga Teacher training with Anne Marie Newland at Sun Power Yoga, and I then went on to do more training with Sports Yoga teacher Sarah Ramsden (the woman who made Ryan Giggs doing yoga famous!) and have a Yoga for Athletes and Sport accreditation, followed by a further 60 hours on The Body Aligned - Yoga, Functional Anatomy and Injury.

I'm also a Total Yoga Nidra Teacher after studying with Uma Dinsmore-Tuli, and have studied Yin Yoga with Norman Blair, Rebecca Shepherd and Rose Shaw. I spent time at Oxford University studying Mindfulness and my teaching style varies from sweaty to snail pace!

I've worked with West Bromwich Albion Football Club first team which was a great experience considering I know nothing about football, and I also have a monthly column in the top national yoga magazine, Om Yoga. I'm an Ambassador for Asquith London, an exclusive yoga clothing brand so hit me up for some discount codes!

Woah Claudia - You certainly know your stuff then when it comes to Yoga! Can you tell us about the benefits of doing Yoga and Meditation in the run up to bedtime?

Getting into a routine to prepare for bedtime is great for the mental signpost that it's time for sleep. Some gentle stretches will also tune into the mind/body connection and ease the body into the parasympathetic nervous system 'relax and restore' mode, rather than the adrenaline pumping, sympathetic nervous system, 'fight or flight' mode.

Yoga will help iron out the kinks of the day, and it is great for both parent and child, especially as a bit of bonding time.

Not all kids like to switch off and chill - So how can parents encourage a reluctant child to give yoga and meditation a go?

A lot of schools are introducing yoga now, so your child may already have had a go at school, so it might be helpful to find out if they are using a particularly DVD or YouTube channel as a good starting point.

You could maybe tempt them with a *chocolate meditation*. Chocolate works for adults and children - I mean who doesn't like chocolate?!

Making up fun names for poses could also help the reluctant child give it a go! I have a sticker reward system in my classes (for reals) when adults get gold star stickers for doing well or improving. This is just as good a motivator for adults as it is for children.

I've actually seen full on sulks in class when people don't get a sticker but their friend does, (these people are in their 40's!) PT Sean once refused a sticker because he thought it was a 'pity sticker'. To be fair, it was.

Brilliant! I love the idea of stickers for adults too! (Even if it does cause grow-up sulks!) I think families would love the competitive side of earning stickers through yoga poses!

Some kids have reward charts for behaviour or household chores at home so this could be a really nice add on - a reward chart for relaxing or doing yoga. To me that sounds like heaven, but kids sometimes need a bit more persuading!

Please tell us more about chocolate yoga! As a chocoholic myself - this sounds awesome!

It's a fun way of quietening the mind and will work well with children and adults alike! This is the script I use with my clients.

You'll need a piece of chocolate for this!

'Chocolate meditation is my favourite kind of meditation'
Oscar age 8

Chocolate Meditation

Sit comfortably and look at the wrapped chocolate -

Does the wrapper make a sound as you move it around in your hand?

What colour is it?

Does it have any words or letters on it? What does it say?

Where did it come from?

Pick up the chocolate and feel the weight of it in your hand

Be aware of the sensation, the feeling of the chocolate in your hand

Now SLOWLY open the chocolate

Do you feel a sense of anticipation, or an urge to immediately put the chocolate in your mouth?

What physical sensations do you have?

What emotions are you feeling? Just note them.

Look at the chocolate

Consider its texture, colour, weight...

Smell the chocolate - does the smell trigger any other senses?

Where do you feel your sense of smell?

Place the chocolate in your mouth but DO NOT EAT IT YET!!

Close your eyes.

How does it feel as it melts?

Where in your mouth can you taste it?

What is the consistency?

What is happening with your mouth, teeth, tongue, lips as it melts?

Move the chocolate around your mouth

Does the area of taste change?

Does the taste itself change?

What is happening to the chocolate?

How do you feel?

Swallow the chocolate, focusing on the sensation.

Is there a lingering taste?

How do you feel physically and emotionally?

Finally, when the chocolate is gone, bring your attention back to your senses.

Notice whether there is still a residual chocolatey taste in your mouth, whether the smells
in your awareness have changed.

Bring your attention back to your breath and to the feelings going on inside you.

Rest for a moment, just breathing, and being aware of how you feel – is it different in any way to how you felt at the start of the meditation?

Bring your attention back to the rest of the room, the sounds you can hear, the cushions or floor beneath you, and the weight of your body on the earth.

When you're ready, open your eyes.

I love this script! What a fun way to meditate without actually realising it!

Let's talk about Yoga poses. Are there certain child-friendly Yoga poses that are helpful for calming a body down and getting ready for rest at night?

Yes! Try this little routine; Lie on your bed or on a yoga mat on the floor if you have one. Bring your knees up to your chest have a little roll around, front to back, side to side or make little circles into your lower back.

Bring your feet down and drop your knees over to one side, then the other like windscreen wipers. Do this 2 or 3 times to each side.

Then take your legs in the air and straighten them as much as you can and then release down and shake out legs (again up to 3 times).

Now lie out on the mat or mattress, take your arms overhead and do a full body stretch, stretching every single muscle and then RELEASE on a big EXHALE and allow your whole body to sink into the mat.

Take a deep breath right down into your tummy, feeling it fill up like a balloon, then slowly exhale relaxing into the mattress. Do this as many times as you like.

Kids (and adults) also respond really well to *Yoga Nidra* which translates as 'conscious sleep' or 'sleep with a trace of awareness' and they are usually themed.

It's a powerful technique in which you learn to relax consciously, using a systematic method of inducing complete physical, mental and emotional relaxation. It is a delicious state of mind in between wakefulness and sleep, and it is the nearest thing you can get to hypnotism without the actual hypnosis!

What about meditation? Can children really do it?

Probably better than adults - they have no preconceived ideas and don't remember Woodstock, The Beatles and Timothy Leary, and aren't really aware of the adults who float about wearing white and chanting Om.

There is so much more to meditation and I think that kind of image really puts people off. The main aim is to quieten the mind, not to silence or 'stop' it - that is impossible! Think of the brain like a muscle that you want to train - the more often you meditate, the better you become at it. Kids tend to just get on with it and not question the process so much.

That's a really good point Claudia! I think the whole hippy idea of meditating comes from movies and the ideas of the 70's, so children are totally unaware of those ideas and approach it all with a fresh head!

What would be your top tips for a simple to follow meditation session for children?

Find a few meditations they like on an App, *YouTube* or download a meditation playlist on *iTunes* or *Spotify*.

Create a meditation space - maybe in the corner of a room, have a special chair or cushions, fairy lights, maybe an air diffuser with an aroma to associate with the practice. Lavender is calming and often associated with relaxation and as a sleep aid.

Have blankets, comfy clothes, or if it's bedtime, PJ's on, and make a really lovely ritual out of it.

I love that idea! The whole thought of that is making me feel relaxed already!

How often (ideally) should children do yoga and/or meditation if it's to work towards aiding better sleep.

It depends on the child and what they have been doing that day and also why they are doing it! If it's a bedroom routine, then every night even just for 5 minutes will help. There are usually yoga classes for kids in your local town, and as I've said, a lot of schools are doing yoga and meditation now.

Are there any apps or online resources you'd recommend parents take a look at?

The Yoga Nidra Network offers free downloads, there's also *Calm For Kids*, and *relax kids* online which offer free resources.

There are quite a few apps such as *Insight Timer* which is free, and *Headspace, Calm* and *Breathe* - which you can pay to upgrade to for the full benefits. I use Headspace because I think it's the best one and I pay for the subscription. They have kids meditations themes you can choose from including:

• Appreciation
• Rest & Relax
• Settling Down
• Goodnight
• Calm
• Kindness
• Paying Attention
• Good Morning
• Cool Off
• Sleep Tight

Available to all subscribers, kids (and their parents) can enjoy fun, engaging activities that teach them the basics of mindfulness. They'll practice breathing exercises, visualisations and even try some focus-based meditation. Of course, different exercises work best for different ages so they've customised the sessions for three age groups: 5 and under, 6-8 and 9-12.

Thanks Claudia - I'm feeling pretty chill after our chat and I'm sure our readers will be encouraged to let their children give yoga and meditation a go, and maybe even try it together as family!

Namaste! (The light in me honours the light in you)

Chapter Nine
The Better Bedroom Brigade - How comfortable surroundings make better sleep spaces.

We've all had that bad night sleep before becoming parents. You know, the sleepover at a friends house where you just can't get comfy? Maybe you've been the second child who got the hand-me-down lumpy mattress from their older sibling, or the kid that had the coldest room in the house?

Maybe you've been a guest at a night over for a family event, lodged between the ironing board and bookcase? (I have to mention here this really awesome hashtag over the festive season of everyone sharing their sleeping spaces. #DuvetknowitsChristmas celebrates all the weird and wonderful ways people fall asleep as they go home for Christmas.)

The annual tradition was started by writer *Rhodri Marsden* a few years ago when he asked for people to submit their worst sleeping situations. Now Rhodri uses the fun hashtag to shed light on a serious issue; Not everyone has a warm room or bed at Christmas, so *Twitter UK* partnered with homelessness charity *Shelter* to raise money to prevent people living on the streets. Isn't that rather lovely? Nice work Rhodri and Twitter UK!

So - you see, it's a no-brainer that to be able to sleep well, you need to be comfortable. (Unless you're my husband who could probably sleep standing up in a hurricane.)

Rather than rattle on about comfort, here's a nice little checklist to getting a better bedroom and thus - better sleep! Tadaa!

Buy a good mattress

Lumpy mattresses are not going to get you a decent night's sleep os if it's past it's best - it's time to shop for a new one. With this in mind, don't even try to comparison shop. Cheap usually means rubbish (take it from this bargain queen who regrets a recent purchase online!)

A good quality mattress should serve you at least 6 years (let's be honest - most don't buy a new mattress for 10,) so splash the cash if you can. It really is worth it.

If ordering online, find a mattress shop that offers the option to 'try for 30 days' (lots of shops do now,) and make sure your child is happy with that mattress. Check it yourself - spend a night in their bed (or at least a little lie down on their bed for a bit.)

Pick out the mattress you think is most comfortable, try it out if you are buying it in a shop and get your child to do the same. The mattress that allows you to sink into a deep, natural sleep and wake up in the morning without aches and pains is the one you want - so if in the shop it feels like it could do this - buy it and keep it.

Invest in good bedding

Fancy bedding isn't needed, but *comfortable* bedding is. Get a good quality quilt and comfortable pillows. Check the tog and change for the time of year.

Choose a nice quilt cover they'll like and more importantly feel safe in. (*Safe Fi? What on earth are you on about love?*) Well, lovely faces - let me share a little story with you (with consent of course - no names though, the child in question is now a 6ft, nineteen year old who won't thank me for publishing his bedtime-dramas now he's all grown up!

This lovely family couldn't fathom why their 6 year old hated bedtime. Tears and tantrums and constant getting out of bed, all came down to one thing. The duvet cover.

The rather awesome Spiderman cover he had chosen - was his favourite superhero, but on the underside of the quilt, it was covered in little spiders! Gross! I don't blame him getting out of bed eleventy-billion times!

A quick change to a plain duvet and he was soon sleeping soundly night after night. So there you go - find a duvet cover they like and feel *safe* and happy in!

Blankets are perfect for chilly nights - if your child gets cold and they have a blanket near by to quickly pop over the top of their duvet, they'll be less likely to get out of bed to tell you they're cold! Blankets are also great for summer when a quilt is too hot but your child still wants to feel secure.

Room temperature

The temperature of the room where your child is sleeping definitely affects your child's sleep so it's worth investing in a room thermometer for younger children. In my book *The Baby Bedtime Book - Say Goodnight to sleepless nights!* I talk about this too.

Your body temperature peaks in the evening and then drops to its lowest levels when you're asleep, so 16-18°C (60-65°F) is thought to be an ideal temperature in a bedroom. Temperatures over 24°C (71°F) are likely to cause restlessness, while a cold room of about 12°C (53°F) will make it difficult to drop off.

Again, blankets are ideal to have near by for children to use as during the light sleep phase (usually around 3am) the body is at a low temperature and they can often wake feeling cold. Reaching for a blanket instead of getting out of bed to come and tell you they're cold means a better sleep for everyone.

Room lighting

Although darkness is best for sleep (because when it's dark, we release melatonin, which relaxes the body.) As mentioned in a previous chapter, many children are afraid of the dark.

Rather than having a pitch-black room, invest in a low light nightlight. A sleep clock, like a *gro-clock*, is ideal for a child's room as it emanates a low blue glow that is just enough to see the pathway to the bathroom but not enough to keep your child awake.

In Summer, when it's bright at your child's bedtime - it's no surprise they may struggle to fall asleep. Black-out blinds are ideal for the spring clock changes, and you can even get stick on temporary ones if your budget is limited. Black out blinds often stop the early-riser finding you at 5am demanding breakfast, or switching Cbeebies or Boomerang on!

The biggest no-no at bedtime when it comes to lighting are mobile phones and computer screens; These LED displays glow with blue light, which suppresses melatonin even more. It's one of the biggest causes of sleep issues that I help knackered parents with.

Bedroom Sounds

I have good hearing and hear the slightest noise in the night and often wake my sleeping husband to tell him! He is always really thankful for this disturbance in his sleep.

Our children however, luckily haven't inherited their Mum's ability to be woken by a mouse walking on the path outside, and sleep soundly, like their dad, through storms, neighbours parties, and once an intruder in the garden that set the dogs off going bonkers. (It's fine - they didn't break in and I think me going down into the kitchen in just my pants and a vest was enough to make them run off and turn away from a life of crime!)

Some children are highly sensitive to noise at night especially sudden or repetitive noises, and these can interrupt sleep and cause real issues night after night. Especially external sounds from the streets outside.

One of the best ways to combat outside noise is double glazing (I sound like a sales person now! I so should've got a sponsorship deal with a window company for this chapter!) Seriously though - good windows really do muffle sounds from outside - take it from someone who lived right on the *South East London, South Circular.* It was worth the investment for a good nights sleep night after night.

If replacing windows and doors (oh my life, I really do sound like a windows sales person,) isn't within your finances, then invest in some good quality ear plugs for your child if you live in a particularly noisy area. Soft foam ear plugs are particularly effective and even drown out snoring (should you have snoring family members,) and other household noises such as noisy boilers, TV noises from Netflix-watching parents and other sounds.

While some like to sleep in perfect peace, others find certain sounds comforting. 'White noise' sounds aren't just beneficial for little babies, older children and even adults, can find the soft whooshing sound quite soothing and helpful for joining the land of nod.

Music, or sounds of forests or seasides, played softly through a small speaker can also help children to feel relaxed and fall asleep.

Bedroom smells

A clean bedroom is a happy bedroom - this is what I tell my little ones and it's kinda sinking in. Well, almost.

To be fair to them, they are pretty cool, and they empty their bins once a week make their beds (definitely not instagram worth bed making skills - but made at least!) They put washing in the laundry bin when reminded and once a fortnight pull off the bedsheets for me to wash and change them (well trained hey?)

Let's face it - smelly sheets are not comfy sheets. Everyone loves clean-sheet day right? Bedroom bins with rotting food are not nice environments to sleep in and it's these simple things that can create a good or bad nights sleep.

One thing I do love is the smell of lavender. I know I've mentioned it already in the *monster spray* - but lavender pillows, lavender reeds and even lavender plug-ins are brilliant for making a bedroom smell and feel relaxing and cosy.

This of course - gets wiped out by the pre-teen bottom burps and sweaty socks, but you can but try, to make the room smell clean and fresh, thus creating the perfect smelling canvas for a great nights sleep.

TV's in children's bedrooms - yes or no?

Getting a good night's sleep is achievable when you take care to not use technology in the bedroom. This means TV's too - so no falling asleep to the TV. It's a big habit that so many parents come to me with! Their children fall asleep beautifully to the TV or iPad, but when they go through the *light sleep phase* they are wide awake. They need help drifting back off because they are used to the noise and comfort the tech brings each night. These kind of 'crutches' mean your child relies on something to help them settle, rather than learning to naturally fall asleep themselves.

My own two have T.V's in their bedrooms - but they don't watch them before bed each night, in fact they rarely switch them on in the evenings, and Tv time is mainly downstairs as a family.

Instead, they watch movies on weekends and sometimes as a treat, have a 'movie night' where they watch a movie in bed with popcorn, then switch off, and get into the sleep zone by reading for a while before going to sleep.

However you choose to 'sleep zone' your child's room - think about everything you've read in this book so far that creates a 'good sleeping environment' and make an informed choice on how to make it a perfect sleeping space for your child. You'll be doing yourself a favour long-term.

Chapter Ten
The Noisy Sleeper - A look into Childhood Snoring and Sleep Apnoea

Snoring partners cause so many sleepless nights (mine included - sorry hun!) But when it comes to children - do you about 10 percent of children snore most nights?

What is snoring?

Snoring is a noise that occurs during sleep when you breath in and there is a blockage of the air passing through the back of the mouth. This creates that hortling-chortling noise that can wake partners or siblings who room share.

The snoring noise itself is caused by the opening and closing of the air passage, which causes a vibration of the tissues in the throat. Sometimes the snoring can be quiet, and sometimes it can be so loud it shakes the house. This is because noise level is affected by how much air is passing and how fast the throat is vibrating.

Snoring tends to occur during the deeper stages of sleep and the 'snorer' won't be aware they are doing it.

Should I worry about snoring?

Although snoring is common, there are some things to look out for if your child is a constant snorer as it could be a sign of something else, such as sleep apnea.

What is sleep apnea?

According to NHS UK, Obstructive Sleep Apnoea (OSA) is a relatively common condition where the walls of the throat relax and narrow during sleep which interrupts normal breathing. This may lead to regularly interrupted sleep, which can have a big impact on quality of life and increases the risk of developing certain conditions.

Contributing factors to sleep apnea may be obesity, allergies, asthma, gastroenterological reflux disorder, an abnormality in the physical structure of the face or jaw as well as medical and neurological conditions.

In children, the most common physical problem associated with sleep apnea is large tonsils. Young children's tonsils are quite large in comparison to the throat, peaking at five to seven years of age. Swollen tonsils can block the airway, making it difficult to breathe and could signify apnea.

What symptoms should I look out for?

- Your child snores loudly and on a regular basis.

- Their breathing has pauses, gasps, and snorts and actually stops breathing. (The snorts or gasps may waken them and disrupt their sleep.)

- Your child is restless during the night or they sleep in abnormal positions with their head in unusual positions.

- They sweat heavily during sleep.

How is OSA diagnosed?

If you suspect your child may have symptoms of sleep apnea, talk to your GP who may refer you to a sleep specialist.

According to Great Ormond Street hospital, (GOSH) once referred, your child will be invited to have a sleep study performed. This is a test performed during an overnight stay in hospital, which measures various body functions, such as breathing pattern and heart rate. This determines the child's sleep quality and breathing pattern.

From the results of the sleep study, the medical professionals associated with the child's care will make a diagnosis of obstructive sleep apnoea.

Undiagnosed and untreated sleep apnea may contribute to daytime sleepiness and behavioural problems including difficulties at school.

What treatments will my child be offered?

Depending on the results of the findings there are a few options available for your child, including:

- An Ear, Nose and Throat (ENT) review - a child may have an appointment with an ENT surgeon to see if there are any problems with the airway that can be corrected with an operation.

- Nasal prongs – this is a soft plastic tube with two prongs that are inserted into the child's nostrils. These help the child's breathing at night by keeping the airway open.

- Continuous Positive Airway Pressure (CPAP) is a continuous flow of air is given to your child through a mask which they will wear at night. This mask helps to maintain their airway and aids in breathing at night. When used correctly every night, the child's sleep quality and daytime symptoms should improve.

For the regular snorers who have had their snoring confirmed as just regular snoring, don't have sleep apnea, there are a few things you can do to help.

Allergies, colds and general illness can bring on bouts of snoring so look into antihistamines, anti allergy bedding or decongestants (always consult your GP or pharmacist on this!)

Elevating your child's head on a thicker pillow can also help.

If siblings share a room and one is a snorer that is keeping them awake, invest in some good quality ear-plugs for them to get a better night's rest.

Remember, snoring and talking or making sounds while asleep, is common, but if you have any real concerns with your child's breathing and snoring during sleep, always contact a medical professional for advice.

Chapter Eleven
Teenage Mutant Ninja sleepers - a look into things to come.

As children approach the teen years, sleep changes considerably!

Your teen will need less sleep, tend to stay awake longer, and sleep-in later. (Yes! I know! It's like a big reward that you actually made it through in one piece the last 13 years!)

A few bits in this chapter may feel a bit repetitive - but I'm sharing them again for the pre-teen and teen parents who may have skipped forward to this chapter for a quick fix!

One thing is for certain when it comes to teenagers - sleep is crucial for them because it's while snoozing, they release a hormone that is essential for their growth spurt. They actually need more sleep than both children and adults, but they actually tend to get less than either!

How much sleep do teenagers need?

Typically teenagers need 9-10 hours of sleep each night. (This means teenagers still need more sleep than adults to be at their best during the day.) The majority of adolescents however, aren't getting nearly as much sleep as they need, and sleep deprivation in teens can be particularly hard on girls.

Dr. Mary Carskadon, a sleep researcher and professor at Brown University, knows how sleep is foundational to health.

'The benefit of sleep is huge. One of the main goals of adolescent development is to learn and to improve their intellectual capacity and adequate sleep affects that,' she says. *'Less sleep means less motivation to learn, slower recall and less retention of information, which means less learning overall.*

Girls can experience some emotional changes during puberty, and the lack of sleep can also affect their overall mood. From acting irritable to acting out, lack of sleep can cause kids to feel depressed, standoffish and generally not themselves.'

It's not just about how much sleep teenagers get. It's also about how well they sleep, and how much *deep sleep* they get. As you know by now, (if you read the start of this little book) this deep sleep is the most restful phase of sleep and the most important part for repair. A lack of sleep can have an effect on moods - and as any parent of a teen knows, mood swings are hard-work at the best of times, so creating healthier sleep will create a healthier teen both physically and mentally.

It's very common for teenagers to want to go to stay up much later, and get up later in the morning. All the years of early wake-ups will be now behind you and you'll be the one dragging your teen out of bed. This is because they start to secrete melatonin later at night than they did in earlier childhood, which affects their circadian rhythm.

How puberty effects sleep:

Puberty plays a large part in sleep habits too, making sleep habits very different from the early childhood years. New research suggests that the hormonal upheaval of puberty could be causing adolescents to love a lie-in, but loathe an early night.

One important change that occurs at night time is increased levels of the 'darkness hormone' melatonin, which helps us to fall asleep. Most adults start to produce melatonin at about 10pm, but when teenagers were studied in a sleep laboratory, researchers discovered that they only began to produce the hormone at 1am.

This delay in melatonin production however, might simply be caused by the behaviour of teenagers.

Teenagers often stay up late, they often play computer games or watch television before sleep. This stimulates the brain and exposes the teenagers to bright lights which could cause the later release of melatonin.

On the other hand, the hormonal upheaval of puberty could be pushing the melatonin release back, in which case teenagers are being kept awake by their bodies - they simply can't help their peculiar sleeping behaviour.

With this new teen sleep research in mind, MPs recently debated whether the school day should start later to allow teenagers to have a lie-in, after an online petition, started by Hannah Kidner, 18, received more than 183,000 signatures! A succession of MPs and teachers supported the student's demand for teenagers to be allowed to start school later, citing various scientific studies which showed it would lead to healthier students.

The debate was opened in the House of Commons (February 2019) by the Cambridge MP Daniel Zeichner. The MPs resolved to 'note the petition' and called for more research to be carried out on the subject.

How can I help my Teenager sleep?

There are lots of simple ways you can help your teenager to get better sleep, and to be totally honest, they aren't that different from the tips for younger children, but bare in mind, that while it's one thing to enforce bedtime for a younger child, when it comes to adolescents, it's a whole different ball-game!

Teenagers aren't likely to change their sleep habits unless they understand and realise that more sleep will make them feel better and improve their performance in school.

Communication is key here, so talk to them on their wavelength and don't nag, (nagging never works!) If as a parent, you've you've skipped ahead to this chapter - and not read the rest, I've share my teen-sleep tips in a nice, snappy format, pointing you to the chapters most relevant for teens.

Set a good example

You're probably not going to want to hear this - but if you want your teen to have better bedtime habits, you need to show them that you have good bedtime habits too! This means no staying up all night watching Netflix, (I know right?!) Ditching the phone at bedtime, and basically creating good examples for them to follow. Hard truth - true story.

It's no good telling them to do one thing and then doing the complete opposite yourself. It may work in the early childhood days, and even the pre-teen days, but teens are a new parenting category. If you want your teen to sleep better, you need to show them how to sleep better yourself or they will just throw your wise sleep words back in your face.

Limit screens in the bedroom

Most teens are attached to their phone. Hey - most adults are! It's kind of normal life these days right? But, as mentioned before, tech at bedtime really isn't great for getting a good nights sleep for anyone.

You know that blue hue coming from your child's phone, TV, and tablet? Did you know it effects their ability to feel satisfied with the sleep they actually get? The light from the device actually suppresses melatonin (the magic stuff that induces the sleepy vibe.)

This hormone supports your sleep/wake cycle known as *circadian rhythm,* so, when your cycle is off, you feel less rested. Switching off from any screen time at least 30 minutes before bedtime will lessen this effect on your circadian rhythm and make your child feel a lot better, so forget the FOMO (Fear of missing out to those not as cool in teen lingo as me) and ditch the tech at bedtime.

Tech Stimulates Your Brain: Depending on what your teen watches on TV, or which the game they play on their games console or phone - any excitement too close to bedtime will keep them up longer than you'd like. Tech stimulates the brain so you want to switch off a good while before bedtime - at least half an hour.

It's the same for sending texts, messages, or scrolling social media. All of these things stimulate the mind just at the moment you're trying to chill and get into the sleepy-vibe you need to fall asleep.

Switch off - not silent: A silent room for sleeping, with no interruptions - is a better sleep space than one that disturbs with phone alerts, phone glow or TV's on low in the background.

Switch off properly, not just silent your teens tech. Even better - make the bedroom a 'no-tech zone' after a certain time. I know one family of tech addicts, used my 'phone ban box' successfully. It's a simple shoe box, in the hallway, that all phones went into past 8pm. Even the adults used it! (ouch - I know - but it works!) all tech off in rooms - TV, tablet, laptop - OFF.

The family switched to old-school alarm clocks for the school wake-up days and noticed a difference in their sleep as a family in only 3 days! The parents felt the benefits too and reported back that mornings were calmer, there was less stress in the house and there was a huge improvement in family time and communication! So you see - sometimes being a little strict with yourself too, can create great rewards.

Exercise for better sleep: Exercise not only keeps your body and weight healthy, it is a magic key to a good nights sleep. Teenagers should be aiming for at least 60 minutes' exercise every day, including aerobic activities such as fast walking and running. Head on over to the *Jump Around* chapter for more details on how exercise helps sleep and tips to get your teenager moving more.

Ditch the caffeine: Teenagers start to drink caffeinated drinks or even start having coffee and tea in the mornings or while studying after school. But did you know that drinking caffeine up to 4 hours before bedtime can cause major problems with sleep? Also too much caffeine can stop them falling asleep altogether.

Bedtime snacks: Snacking too closely to bedtime can lead to an overfull stomach and make falling asleep tricky. Encourage your teen to eat a well balanced diet, avoid snacking in favour of proper meals, and avoid too much sugary food, especially before bedtime.

Routine is the magic key: Just like the baby and toddler days - routine really does help create better sleep habits, so encourage your teenager to get into a regular bedtime routine. Encourage them to have a bath, maybe read a book in favour of the tech, and have a warm milky drink each night.

A consistent sleep schedule will help your teen to feel less tired since it allows their body to get in sync with its natural patterns. These good sleep routines will really help them through exam times when good sleep is essential for study.

Better bedrooms: Check out my chat on creating a better sleep space in the "" chapter. A better, peaceful (and clean) sleep space will hop your teenager fall asleep and stay asleep - getting them the much needed 8-9 hours they need.

Communication is key: Your teen may have trouble falling asleep due to worries or anxieties. Make a weekly appointment where you take time to chat together.

Take them out for one-on-one time so they can open up and share anything they're worried about. This will help them to put their problems into perspective and sleep better.

If your teen is a reluctant talker, invest in a journal where they can leave messages for you - share what they are feeling without being judged or told off.

Avoid long lie-ins: We all love a lie-in, but late nights and late mornings can create a bad sleep-pattern so encourage your teen to not sleep in for hours on end at weekends.

This doesn't mean waking them at 7am on a Saturday, but aim to get them up before 10am to promote better sleep patterns throughout the week.

Finally, when it comes to your teen - remember, not getting enough sleep can lead to chronic sleep deprivation. This can have dramatic effects on their life by impacting their mental wellbeing, increasing their risk of depression, anxiety and low self-esteem. It can also affect academic performance at school - a time when it is most important, especially where exams are involved.

With this in mind, don't feel like the bad guy when it comes to enforcing certain bedtime rules. By creating better sleep patterns - you are doing them a huge favour (even if they may not see it that way at first!)

My experiences of teenagers over the years, have taught me many things, but mainly that you need to work together towards a plan rather than nagging with a list of bedtime rules. Just because your teen has outgrown time-out or sticker charts, it doesn't mean you can't create effective consequences or offer privileges for following the simple house rules.

Incentives such as more time out with friends on weekends for positive behaviour, or tech bans and grounding for negative responses - are great ways of getting your teen onboard when it comes to bedtime rules.

Be realistic though - their friends are likely to be up late too, and peer pressure is enormous in the online world, so come to an agreement of what is a reasonable 'switch off' time and relax/sleep time that you all agree on as a family and stick to it.

Hopefully, if you work together and are on the same page, you'll create great sleep habits that your teen will take into adult life.

Chapter Twelve
When to get help: Childhood Behavioural Sleep Problems - when and where to go for professional help.

Sometimes, *Wide Awake Kids Club* members need a little bit more help than you can manage or deal with. In these instances it is worth seeking help from a trained professional to help you.

Reasons may include:

- **Behavioural insomnia:** Parents have problems setting limits, and dealing with their child around bedtime resulting in poor sleep health and stress.

- **Delayed sleep phase:** Children go to bed late and wake late or need to be woken by their parents.

- **Anxiety-related insomnia:** Worries and anxieties make falling asleep near impossible

- **Parasomnias:** Abnormal movements, behaviours, emotions, perceptions, and dreams that occur while falling asleep

- **Movement disorders in sleep:** including periodic limb movement disorder (PLMD) which is repetitive cramping or jerking of the legs during sleep

- **Circadian rhythm disorders:** Disruptions to a child's circadian rhythm - a name given to the "internal body clock"

- **Sleep disordered breathing:** (SDB) is a general term for breathing difficulties occurring during sleep. SDB can range from frequent loud snoring to Obstructive Sleep Apnea (OSA)

- **Narcolepsy:** A neurological disorder that affects the control of sleep and wakefulness.

- **Kleine-Levin syndrome:** (KLS), is a rare sleep **disorder** characterised by persistent episodic hypersomnia and cognitive or mood changes.

- **Idiopathic and secondary hypersomnia:** A neurological disorder which is characterised primarily by excessive daytime sleepiness (EDS)

If your child's sleeping problems haven't been resolved by trying my gentle techniques and guidance in this book, and you have real concerns for certain sleep behaviours or are worried there is something troublesome about their sleeping patterns, then it is important to seek extra help from your GP or qualified sleep professional.

Please remember there is absolutely nothing to feel ashamed of or be embarrassed by, when it comes to asking for help as a parent. Sleep is an incredibly difficult thing to master and nobody will judge you for seeking extra help.

Where can I get extra help?

Talk to your GP who may suggest you make an appointment at a children's sleep clinic, if there's one in your area.

The Children's Sleep Disorder Service is a specialist centre for children's sleep but there are only a few in the UK. They work with children aged between 1 and 18 who have chronic sleep disorders, who have already been seen by their GP or at another hospital and been referred.

Private help:

There are lots of trained sleep professionals online who offer private sleep packages to help you with your child's sleep issues, some of my absolute faves, who I've had the privilege of working with over the years, I've shared at the back of this book.

Please be aware, that there are many *'parenting experts'* and *'sleep experts'* out there that have no qualifications or experience, so do check references, recommendations and choose wisely before booking a consultation.

Online help:

There are lots of lovely resources for parents online so I've checked out a few and put the super-helpful ones below.

- The Children's Sleep charity - www.thechildrenssleepcharity.org.uk

- The sleep Council - www.sleepcouncil.org.uk

Chapter Thirteen
Night-night from Fi!
(Do you practice what you preach?)

Honestly? Yes I do - but not just for my little ones and their wellbeing - it's for my wellbeing too! It's about quality time and 'switch-off' time from being a mum! (It's also about having a good old Netflixathon, dinner and a cheeky Vimto in peace.

My two are currently (as I write this,) 8 and 9 years old. We get up at 6.30am every school morning (I have to wake them most mornings,) and they both have the same bedtime each night.

They go to bed around 7pm on *most* school nights, then they read until 7.30pm when I shout up to them to turn their reading lights off. So, mostly, that's a total of around 11 hours SLEEP each night but 11 1/2 hours in bed resting.

On footy or *Brownies* nights, or at weekends, it's usually an 8-830pm bedtime, (If they stay at Nanna and Poppops, if we go away, or if there's a family party, then of course - it's much, much later!)

These late nights are few and far between as I have learned valuable lessons from experience. Any regular break in the routine usually has consequences! They are always shattered and very grumpy the next morning.

I've come to realise that even though they aren't babies anymore - they still really need their sleep, and their routine and it's why I always insist on the early bedtime on other nights. If you look at the guidance chart - they are actually getting (mostly) what they should. It's a fair compromise - and because they're reading until 8pm, they rarely complain about the 7pm 'into-bed now' routine.

In all honesty - sometimes we have times when bedtime isn't a nice time. The bad moods, over tiredness, arguments or messing about can make it a pretty stressful time, but the majority of nights, nine times out of ten, they go to bed, they read quietly and they go to sleep when it's lights-out time, (if they haven't already fallen asleep.)

People say I'm lucky I have good sleepers, but I honestly don't think it's about luck. It's about routine, consistency and hard work in the early years, it's also about not slipping into bad routines which can be so easily done - especially in the summer when the weather is nice and you lose track of time in the garden.

The thing I always say to parents is there is no right or wrong way to approach sleep as a parent. You do what works for you and your family.

If you still love to co-sleep with your 4 year old, if you love your 9 year old staying up with you until 9.30pm every night, if you don't mind your 7 year old coming into your bed every night at 3am - then it is nobody's business but yours. If you are all happy and getting good sleep then why should it matter?

What I'm saying is, you should always make an informed choice when it comes to your child's sleep; Do makes you happy or gets you and your child the most sleep at the time. Maybe you are having a few problems but don't feel ready to tackle them just yet - that's cool. This book is ready to pick up and put down anytime.

I'm always around on social media if you just need a reassuring *'hey - you got this! Trust your instincts!'* message from me.

Finally, thank you so much for buying this little sleep guide of mine. I really hope you've enjoyed it and it has offered reassurance, guidance and a little humour. But above all - I hope it brings you the gift of sleep.

Much love,

Fi xx

Chapter Fourteen

The Wide Awake Kids Club Captain Credentials - Lovely endorsements from parents and professionals!

I've always wanted to be a captain - I never got to captain the netball team or even the school running team, so here I am head of the Wide Awake Kids Club making myself a captain! (All the LOL's!)

I've been fortunate enough to work with many wonderful families, high profile parents, celebrities and professionals over the years, and thought it might be beneficial (so you can see if this stuff in my book actually works,) to ask them to share their experiences of my advice.

I paid them all a squillion quid each obviously, to say ace things about me, meaning even if you bought this cheap-as chips guide, I'll be forever paying off these people with the profits. Don't feel bad for me though. Just pop a nice review on Amazon and it'll be a bestseller in no time, and I'll soon be debt free from these scoundrels.

Here's what a few of them had to say...

'I've known Fi personally and professionally for many years. She's widely respected within the childcare and early years field, known for her professionalism, trusted in her area of expertise and, most of all, her approachable nature. BAPN members are aware of her amazing work and tell us how they use her website 'Childcare is Fun!' as their recommended 'go to guide' for the parents they work for, in particular new and sometimes anxious mums and dads.

I'm thrilled to be endorsing Fi's latest book and just know everyone who reads it will feel they know Fi and will benefit hugely from all they'll take from within it.'

- Tricia Pritchard, MD BAPN (The Professional Association for Professional Nannies)

'Fi Star-Stone is a regular contributor for Mother&Baby giving her invaluable and expert advice on all things sleep, toddlers and parenting. Her sleep tips are a must-read for any parent!'

- Aimee Jakes, Digital Editor, Mother & Baby

'Good sleep is just as important for older children as it is for babies and this is a clear, practical guide, to ensuring your child gets all the sleep they need. There is something to suit all parenting styles to lead the way to a good night's sleep for the whole family.'

- Nicola Watson, Child Sleep Consultant, BA (Hons)

'Fi has been the ear I've needed when I've doubted everything I thought I knew about being a parent. She doesn't judge and speaks (honestly) from her own experiences as a mother'

- Kate, Mum of one from same-sex blog 'Lesbemums'

'Fi has been so great offering advice to me at several stages in the last few years. She provides ongoing support, really takes on board any problems and offers relevant and helpful advice which has helped us out so much.

She has a wealth of knowledge on sleep issues and this has been invaluable at times when I did not know where to turn.

- Lisa Hodson, Mum of Two

'Fi has an extensive knowledge and experience of childcare spanning over many years, and now with her own two children. Her kindness comes through in the way she offers advice and help without judgment or preaching.

Fi's books are the perfect 'go to' for all parents. I adore Fi and her gentle approach to parenting.'

- *Kelly Shrehorn -Mum of Five.*

'Knowing Fi is like having a parenting guardian angel around in your time of need or even just for a lighthearted parenting chuckle. My motherhood goddess with so much zest for life & supporting others that is comfort blanket we all need at the end of the day to tell you, mama you've got this.'

- Rosie B, Juggling Mum of three under three!

'Fi has a wealth of knowledge, and her non-judgmental attitude means you can literally ask her anything! This comes across in her books and they are great for advice when it comes to a troublesome toddler or even just a bit of reassurance everything will be OK!'

- Ceri Watt Mum of Two

'Fi's practical advice and guidance was a much needed support to us when our son wouldn't sleep. Her sleep tips helped us enormously!'

- Emma Shilton, Mum of Two, blogger at 'Life According to Mrs Shilts'

'Fi is a true inspiration in so many ways..

The most incredible mum! Her zest for life and positivity just shines through everything she does.

I love the way she makes anything seem possible even in tough times - makes me realise that we can make our dreams happen with the right attitude.

A heart of gold and a love for helping people and being the best mum and version of herself at all times. What is there not to love!

Thank you Fi, for all your positivity and for being you! You rock!'

- Laura Chelmick, Professional Nanny, (Professional Nanny of The Year 2005) Maternity Nurse and Mum to be

'A modern, individual, realistic parenting guru!'

- Steve Camsell, Uncle of Three

I have had the pleasure of knowing Fi for many years now and she has been an invaluable help with all 3 of my children over my 10 year parenting journey.

Both my boys have sleep apnea, so sleep has always been quite an issue for us in our household but in particular Fi has been my middle of the night support when I felt I was at a loss.

Our eldest son is severely disabled and does not produce Melatonin, Fi time after time has researched to find ways to help Grayson and I to find ways to help him sleep when his body tells him not to.

She is our real life Mary Poppins at the end of a message and her first book (as I am sure this one) has been picked up by us many many times.'

- Kara Spencer - Mum of Three

'The main difference about Fi's parenting advice, compared to other popular parenting experts, is that she understands that all children are different and that parents are also often very different to each other too. She knows that a regimented sleep, feed, activity routine might not work for your child and that you might not want to do it this way. She understands that some parents love to co-sleep and some can't wait to get their children into their own room as soon as possible. No matter what type of person and parents you are, if you have a spirited child or sensitive little soul, Fi will help to find a way that works for you and your child. Her style of writing is friendly, straight forward, and easy to read. Reading her books are like being given advice by your best mate who has ten children herself and knows a solution for everything! If you want a fail-safe book ti help your little guy or gal get to sleep and stay asleep, then buy Fi's book!

Ruth Dean - Infant school teacher and mum of hilarious 5 year old future entertainer

References

- National Institute of Neurological Disorders and Stroke (NINDS)

- The Common Sense Media Census: Media Use by Tweens and Teens - 2018

- UK National Health Service (NHS)

- The Organisation for Economic Co-operation and Development (OECD)

- The Guardian Online: *Too many children being prescribed melatonin to aid sleep, May 2017*

- Dr. Mary Carskadon, *The Importance of Sleep During Puberty, Always.com*

- Metro online: *Students could soon start school at 10am as MPs back campaign, Feb 2019*

- Dr. David Lewis, University of Sussex

- Young Minds - www.youngminds.org.uk

- You Minds Parents Helpline - 0808 802 5544

- Childcare is Fun (Fi's main website) - www.childcareisfun.co.uk

- The Regular Parent (Fi's podcast and book site) - www.theregularparent.co.uk

- PT Sean Dawson - www.fit4you.org.uk

- Yoga Teacher Claudia Brown

- Tricia Pritchard BAPN - www.bapn.org.uk

- Mother & Baby Magazine - www.motherandbaby.co.uk

- Lesbemums Parenting Blog - www.lesbemums.com

- Hollybobs Parenting Blog - www.hollybobbs.co.uk

- Life According to Mrs Shilts - Parenting and lifestyle blog www.mrsshilts.co.uk

- kellysvintagemakes - kellysvintagemakes.blogspot.com

- Laura Chelmick - 'For you and your Baby' Facebook, instagram and Twitter

- Kara Spencer - Parenting and lifestyle Blog -www.innocentcharmchats.co.uk

Child Sleep Consultants recommended by Fi

- **Nicola Watson** www.childsleepsolutions.co.uk

During her diverse career, Nicola has helped countless children, their parents and carers to get a better night's sleep. She has a BA (Hons) in Social Science and Psychology and is an OCN accredited Child Sleep Consultant.

Nicola is a member of the professional body the British Sleep Society and the Sleep Professionals Association as well as the Child Psychology Group. Nicola has written articles on sleep for the NCT and has trained both parents and professionals on teaching babies and children to sleep through the night.

But perhaps most significantly Nicola is herself a mother who really understands the importance of a good night's sleep to families and most importantly to the child. Nicola is based in Chislehurst, South East London/Kent in the UK.

- **Jo Tantum** www.JoTantum.com

With nearly 30 years experience working with babies and parents worldwide, it's no wonder Jo Tantum is the one of the UK's leading Baby Sleep Experts. Jo is passionate about teaching babies how to love sleeping, with calm, gentle, guidance - all with no tears!

Jo's bestselling book *Baby Secrets* has helped families around the world and she also offers email, phone and Skype support. Jo's *Sleep Angel's* are a team of gentle sleep trainers, and offer overnight 'Rescue Packages' via her website.

You have probably seen Jo at one of The Baby Shows around the country, as one of their key speakers or on Daybreak as their Baby Expert. Jo has also appeared on ITN news, BBC Radio, and in many popular parenting magazines.

Most importantly, Jo is a mother herself, so understands the importance of sleep for all the family.

Jo is based in The Midlands, in the UK.

**DEAREST BETSY-BOO, THANK YOU FOR YOUR HARD WORK IN
PROVIDING THE ILLUSTRATIONS AND COVER DESIGN FOR THIS BOOK.
LOTS OF LOVE MUMMY XX**

ABOUT THE AUTHOR

As a mum of two little ones born less than a year apart, Fi Star-Stone knows that parenting isn't always easy. Her gentle techniques and approachable manner are popular with families and celebrities worldwide and many parents refer to her as 'the nice expert!'

Fi is a qualified parenting advisor with over 25 years working with children and families. Her qualifications include a Degree in Childhood and Youth studies, an NNEB in Nursery nursing, and a Diploma in Childhood studies.

Her bestselling book *The Baby Bedtime Book - Say goodnight to Sleepless Nights'* has been helping parents to give their little ones the gift of happy sleep worldwide!

In 2005 and 2006 Fi was 'highly commended' by The Professional Association of Nursery Nurses for her work with children in her role as a professional Nanny. Fi writes for parenting magazines and websites and is often on BBC radio talking all things parenting, she's also recently joined the fire-service as an on-call fire-fighter!

Likes: Moomins, Cake and kitchen dancing.

Dislikes: Very early mornings and unkind people.

Favourite Music: The Killers, Pink, and David Bowie.

Follow Fi:

Twitter @FiStarStone
Instagram @FiStarStone
Facebook Childcare is Fun!
YouTube: Fi Star-Stone
Podcast: 'The Regular Parent'
available on iTunes
#TheRegularParent
Press enquiries:
fi@Childcareisfun.co.uk

ABOUT THE ILLUSTRATOR

Betsy Stone is 9 years old and is often found with her head in a book, (usually one by her favourite author Jacqueline Wilson.) When she's not reading - she's drawing, and this talent comes from her artist Nanna who paints amazing pictures and talented Daddy who can draw rather epic Marvel characters.

Betsy lives with her mum, dad, brother, two cats and two dogs. She also has approximately 231 snails in the garden - all of which she has named Barbara. (True story!)

Betsy's illustrations are inspired by her favourite illustrator Nick Sharratt, who she would like to be like when she grows up. She would also like to play for Liverpool FC's first team. (Betsy currently plays for her local girls team and is quite the enthusiastic defender and goaly!)

Likes: Football, drawing, writing, playing guitar and reading

Dislikes: Mushrooms and Broccoli.

Favourite Music: Little Mix, Sia, and David Bowie.

Follow Betsy:
You can't - she's too little!

Illustration enquiries:
Fi@childcareisfun.co.uk

The Wide Awake kids Club - Simple Solutions for knackered Parents

Copyright © 2019 Fi Star-Stone

The information provided in this book is designed to provide helpful information on the subjects discussed. This book is not meant to be used, nor should it be used, to diagnose or treat any medical condition. For diagnosis or treatment of any medical problem, consult your own medical professional. The publisher and author are not responsible for any specific health or allergy needs that may require medical supervision and are not liable for any damages or negative consequences from any treatment, action, application or preparation, to any person reading or following the information in this book. References are provided for informational purposes only and do not constitute endorsement of any websites or other sources. Readers should be aware that the websites listed in this book may change.

The Regular Parent Series

The Wide Awake Kids club - is the first book in Fi Star-Stone's *The Regular Parent*' series. More titles in the series will be out soon!

The Regular Parent Podcast is available now on iTunes

The Regular Parent Podcast project - by Fi Star-Stone
I was overwhelmed by the amount of messages and emails I had received over the past few months from worried parents who felt their lives were not 'normal.'

So many feel they are 'not enough' when scrolling through 'instagram perfect' pics, so I decided to start this little project to show them (and the listener,) that every family is different, every child is different, and every parent is different.

That a regular parent – is a parent like you and like me, your life is 'your kind of normal,' and you shouldn't compare it to others. I'm delighted that so many lovely parents have wanted to be involved and I can't wait to share with you this wonderful series of podcasts.

'The Regular Parent' series, takes a look at parenting from the eyes of *regular parents* like you and me. Weekly podcast interviews with real 'everyday' parents and the everyday amazing things they do. So grab yourself a cuppa (or a glass of something nice,) curl up on the sofa and listen to our lovely, regular families share their lives.

From single parents holding down full time jobs and juggling it all, to parents who have little ones with disabilities – 'The Regular Parent' aims to bring all parents together in this new podcast series looking at the lives of regular parents, like you, and like me from all around the world.

The Regular Parent Podcast is available to listen to on iTunes and via the Regular Parent website www.TheRegularParent.co.uk

29704254R00061

Printed in Great
Britain
by Amazon